1·75

Political Parties in Britain
1783–1867

LANCASTER PAMPHLETS

Political Parties in Britain
1783–1867

Eric J. Evans

METHUEN · LONDON AND NEW YORK

First published in 1985 by
Methuen & Co. Ltd
11 New Fetter Lane,
London EC4P 4EE

Published in the USA by
Methuen & Co.
in association with Methuen, Inc.
29 West 35th Street,
New York NY 10001

Typeset in Great Britain by
Scarborough Typesetting Services
and printed by
Richard Clay (The Chaucer Press)
Bungay, Suffolk

British Library Cataloguing in
Publication Data

Evans, Eric J.
Political parties in Britain:
1783–1867 – (Lancaster pamphlets)
1. Political parties – Great Britain –
   History – 18th century
2. Political parties – Great Britain –
   History – 19th century
I. Title   II. Series
324.241' 009   JN1119

ISBN 0–416–37400–X

Contents

Foreword

Lancaster Pamphlets offer concise and up-to-date accounts of major historical topics, primarily for the help of students preparing for Advanced Level examinations, though they should also be of value to those pursuing introductory courses in universities and other institutions of higher education. They do not rely on prior textbook knowledge. Without being all-embracing, their aims are to bring some of the central themes or problems confronting students and teachers into sharper focus than the textbook writer can hope to do; to provide the reader with some of the results of recent research which the textbook may not embody; and to stimulate thought about the whole interpretation of the topic under discussion.

At the end of this pamphlet is a list of the recent or fairly recent works that the writer considers most relevant to the subject.

Acknowledgement

Thanks are due to my co-editor, David King, whose characteristically careful scrutiny of my text produced numerous helpful suggestions. Both his eye for detail and his overall insight into what makes for clarity of exposition have been much appreciated.

EJE
Hornby
May 1985

Note

A number in brackets in the text indicates reference to a work in the 'Further reading' section.

Political Parties in Britain
1783–1867

Introduction

People living in Britain in the last quarter of the twentieth century are accustomed to a political system in which power is exercised by the leaders of that political party which currently holds the greatest number of seats in the House of Commons. These seats are contested, usually at four- or five-year intervals, in general elections at which almost all persons of eighteen years and over are entitled to vote. The general election selects individuals. However, political party organization and discipline are so extensive that it is almost impossible for a candidate to be elected who does not represent a major party. In effect, individuals are elected in a party, not a personal capacity. When they get to Westminster they are expected to vote according to party loyalty rather than personal preference or conviction when these clash. A highly developed system of 'party whips' ensures that, in most instances, the Commons votes on party lines. Thus effective power is vested in the party rather than in a collection of individuals. Political parties are all-important. We even speak of a two-party system of government, implying that the struggle for power is between two leading parties in the state who alternate in government. Since the 1920s these have been the Conservative and Labour parties. Such a description might seem ill suited to a situation in which the electorate spreads nearly all its votes between three parties not two. Yet the 'first-past-the-post' system, in which the successful candidate needs only one more vote than his nearest rival, however many candidates there may be, greatly advantages the two largest parties at the expense of the third. Thus, in the 1983 general election, the Liberal-Social Democratic Alliance

1

achieved 26 per cent of the popular vote which, evenly spread across the constituencies, won only 23 seats. The Labour party, with 28 per cent of the total vote, heavily concentrated in areas of its greatest support, won 209 seats. Somewhat precariously, therefore, the two-party system of government survived into the mid-1980s expressed in terms of influence in the Commons. Such a system was a recognizable feature of British political life in 1867.

This pamphlet seeks to explain how a recognizably modern system of government emerged between 1783 and 1867. In strict constitutional theory, power is shared between three elements – monarchy, Lords and Commons – and at the beginning of our period the first two of these elements had a larger role to play. In some instances this old system still impinges on the new. Parliamentary bills require passage by the House of Lords and ratification by the monarch before they carry the force of law. The powers of the upper House have been severely circumscribed in the twentieth century. It can now delay legislation but not permanently reject it. Few ministers of consequence, except the Lord Chancellor who presides over the judiciary, sit in it and the granting of a peerage to a senior politician usually indicates retirement from active politics. The House of Lords is an elegant talking shop. It sometimes improves parliamentary bills by revising them, but it lacks real power.

The same can be said of the monarchy. The monarch still retains a theoretical right to reject legislation passed by parliament. Since no king or queen in the nineteenth or twentieth centuries has been foolish enough to exercise this right, it has not been necessary to remove a sanction considered essential in late Stuart England but not actually used since 1708. The monarch also retains the right to appoint ministers – they are still called ministers of the crown – to dissolve parliament and to call a general election. In practice, the monarch chooses as prime minister the leader of that party with a Commons majority and invariably accepts the advice of the outgoing prime minister about the timing of a dissolution, thus giving the party in power the substantial advantage of choosing the most favourable date for the next general election. The monarchy is now valued not for its power but for the exercise of its dignified and ceremonial functions.

King, Lords and Commons in late eighteenth-century Britain

Political and constitutional practice were very different two hundred or so years ago. No government fell because of a general election. After

1716 a new House of Commons required to be elected only every seven years and few general elections were called ahead of time. No Hanoverian government lost an election until the Duke of Wellington did so in 1830, during the political crisis which led to the passage of the first Reform Act. When significant electoral changes took place, they were usually in the government's favour. Elections might serve to confirm the monarch's choice of minister and strengthen his position in the Commons. The most spectacular example of this came in March 1784 when George III's new prime minister, the younger Pitt, was given a majority by the electorate which he had previously lacked.

The electorate was much less representative in the late eighteenth century. In England and Wales no more than 10–12 per cent of adult males had the vote; in Scotland and Ireland the proportions were even lower. Most electors were landowners and many large towns did not elect members of parliament of their own (12). Even when men possessed the right to vote, it was far from certain that they would get the chance to exercise it. Only about 30 per cent of seats were contested at elections before 1832; the majority of MPs were returned unopposed as nominees either of great aristocratic families or of the crown. The largest category of MP in the Commons at this time comprised the relatives of the peerage, most of them peers' sons. In the 1784 parliament, for example, 107 of the 558 MPs were sons of peers, or Irish peers who could sit in the Commons. Sixty-eight were close relatives, grandsons, brothers and the like. A further 129 were either baronets (effectively hereditary titled commoners below the rank of the peerage) or closely related to them. Thus, about 55 per cent of MPs at the beginning of our period were from titled families. This family connection can be emphasized in another way. In most eighteenth-century parliaments, roughly one-half of the members of the Commons had fathers who had previously served there or were still doing so.

It might be thought that, with such extensive indirect influence over the Commons, the peers did not need a powerful House of Lords to carry out their wishes. Indeed, the powers of the Lords had perceptibly lessened during the seventeenth century and the House of Lords was the junior house by the 1780s in all but hierarchical status. The main reason for this was that the Commons under the Stuarts (1603–1714) had won the right to the control of taxation and broad financial policy. The House which disposed of funds was bound to be pre-eminent. The Lords, however, had no need to feel threatened by House of Commons supremacy, as the figures above surely indicate. Well beyond 1832, Britain would elect parliaments dominated by landowners rather than by manufacturers, traders or bankers, while no working man would put his bottom on the lush, green seats of the Commons until 1874.

The Lords as a body still retained considerable influence. This was most apparent in the personnel of successive governments. Between 1784 and 1820, according to Professor Cannon's calculations, 43 of the 65 men who achieved Cabinet office were peers, while 14 of the remaining 22 were peers' sons. Not until Palmerston's government of 1859–65 would peers be in a minority in the Cabinet. Most prime ministers, it is true, were commoners since prime ministerial authority was better exercised in the lower House where divisions were frequently sharper and where public opinion counted for more. Nevertheless, the Earl of Liverpool's administration (1812–27) was the longest of the nineteenth century and was led successfully enough from the Lords. The Earl of Salisbury, prime minister three times (1885–6; 1886–92; 1895–1902), showed that the trick could still be managed into the twentieth century.

Of the two Houses, the Lords was much the easier for a government to control. Until the younger Pitt's new creations in the 1780s the peerage was less than 200 strong and regular attenders were substantially fewer. Many 'regulars' were in receipt of 'places of profit' which they held under the crown; these would normally be expected to support the government. For much of the eighteenth century the twenty-six bishops of the Church of England came under this description. Princes of the church were selected at least as much on grounds of political loyalty as on those of personal piety. Then, as now, doctrinal uniformity hardly came into it. Control of the House of Lords, coupled with infrequent and usually trouble-free elections, were the main reasons for the long period of political stability under George I and George II (1714–27 and 1727–60) known as the Whig Oligarchy.

That stability, already subjected to wartime strains during the later 1750s, collapsed under George III. The new king, a young man of only twenty-two at his accession, was determined to reassert the powers of the monarchy and, in doing so, to reduce those of the great Whig landowners who had effectively ruled Britain for two generations. Struggles between the king and the Whig politicians were frequent in the 1760s, resulting in short, unstable ministries. The central issue was the right of the monarch, constitutionally preserved by the Revolution Settlement of 1689, to choose whatever ministers he wished. This clashed with the now well-established practice that such ministers must have, or be able speedily to acquire, majorities in both Houses of Parliament in order to govern. For twelve years (1770–82) George III seemed to have found in Lord North a minister both acceptable to himself, as not being a member of the tainted 'Whig gang', and able to win majorities in the Commons. But the most tenacious opposition grouping, known as the Rockingham Whigs after their leader the Marquis of Rockingham, mounted a firm challenge. They could use a major new political issue, the rights of the American colonists and the War of Independence (1776–83), on which strong opinions were held both inside parliament and in the country at large, to raise the temperature and sharpen the focus of debate. As debts mounted and it became obvious that the war would be lost, North lost control of the Commons and was finally brought to resignation.

The two years from March 1782 to March 1784 saw high political drama and controversy. They demonstrated two central facts about the nature of political power in Britain. First, the different elements in the House of Commons were very difficult to weld into a stable majority. Family interest groups frequently clashed and elements of party organization, though developing rapidly, were not strong enough to claim control for any one group. A large minority of the Commons, numbering substantially more than a hundred, were 'independent country gentlemen'. They usually represented the county seats, which carried superior status and were less associated with corrupt 'interest' and 'management'. These MPs prided themselves on representing their landowning constituents and on rejecting any party associations whatsoever. They had a general predisposition to support government, but that support could never be relied upon and was particularly unpredictable during periods of instability and, as in 1782–3, when the king was at odds with his ministers.

The second central fact was the power which the king still retained. George III, resentful at losing Lord North, was beside himself with fury when, in the spring of 1783, his former trusted prime minister formed an association with the Rockingham Whigs, effectively led by Charles James Fox since Rockingham's death the previous year. With no other administration then possible on grounds of parliamentary arithmetic the king was forced to accept the 'infamous' Fox–North Coalition, but he regarded it from the start as an insult to his royal prerogative. He schemed against his own ministers and used royal influence in the House of Lords to dislodge them. Royal 'placemen' were instructed as to the king's wishes and majorities for the coalition in the Lords dwindled rapidly. When, under sustained and venomous royal prompting, the Fox–North Coalition was twice defeated there in three days in mid-December 1783, the king dismissed it. He replaced it with a ministry headed by William Pitt, whose father had been prime minister

5

for periods in the 1750s and 1760s. The younger Pitt was only twenty-four years old and had been in the Commons for less than three years. In the king's eyes, his main recommendations were his very limited association with established political leaders and the obvious fact that he owed his elevation to royal influence. As to age, the king could reflect that he had been two years younger than Pitt when he acceded to the throne.

The younger Pitt's promotion was, therefore, a clear exercise of independent royal power. What followed in the next three months proved that that power extended beyond mere selection of a prime minister. Pitt had no Commons majority; indeed, he was opposed there by an unprecedentedly cohesive grouping of ex-ministers and their supporters (about 220 in all) baying for blood. His opponents, led by Fox, North and the Duke of Portland, believed that George III was breaking with constitutional precedent by selecting a prime minister without reference to the wishes of parliament, and they now relished the prospect of humbling the young upstart on the floor of the Commons.

This did not happen. Pitt's opponents misjudged both their man and the powers still available to the crown. The new prime minister's obvious steadfastness and growing competence in the face of both baiting and adverse votes won the admiration of many independents in the Commons. The majorities against him began to dwindle. Furthermore, Pitt's reputation both as a reformer and as a new broom who might sweep away the cosy and sometimes squalid political cliques proved popular in the counties and larger English towns where public opinion was becoming more important. When George III used another of his constitutional prerogatives and dissolved parliament three years earlier than the septennial convention required, he was handsomely rewarded. He appealed to the electorate to support Pitt against an opposition which he branded as 'a desperate faction' designing to 'reduce the sovereign to a mere tool in its hands' and the electorate responded fulsomely. In March 1784, Foxites were routed both in the larger constituencies, where opinion among propertied Englishmen could be tested, and in many of the smaller ones where John Robinson, George's election agent, expertly manipulated royal influence. 'Fox's Martyrs', as they were jocularly called by a literate press with memories of the Reformation, numbered about ninety who failed to reappear in the new parliament and Pitt obtained the sound Commons majority he needed. It seemed that the king's interpretation both of his constitutional role and of his choice of minister had been spectacularly upheld.

Party and party ideology to 1789

The 1784 election offers a neat paradox. It showed clearly enough that the rights of the monarch in the political system could both be asserted and sustained. Pitt, the king's choice, had been triumphantly endorsed by the electorate. Yet the king's battles with his political opponents had caused those opponents to refine and develop the notion of party against which George III had ranged himself. Fox's supporters now began to challenge the royal prerogative with organization, propaganda and a clear platform. Their tactics anticipated later party developments. It may even be, as Professor Cannon has suggested, that the king needed to fight fire with fire by marshalling his own anti-Foxite forces on party lines. Court politicians organized supporters, made arrangements for like-minded MPs to vote together and used propaganda to influence the electorate. An anti-party monarch had to organize a party to defeat his opponents. In the long term, as we shall see, party would expand to fill the vacuum in political life left as royal influence began to decline from the end of the eighteenth century. The king's victory in 1783–4 had many pyrrhic elements.

Party in 1783 was already over a century old. The terms Whig and Tory came into use in the later 1670s to describe the views of those respectively for and against the exclusion of Charles II's Catholic brother, James, Duke of York (later James II), from legitimate succession to the throne. On the Whig side, party stressed the institution of parliament as a necessary brake on royal power; on the Tory side, it implied a defence of established institutions and, in particular, those of the monarchy. A pro-Whig writer concluded in the 1770s that the 'most material doctrine' of the early Tories was 'to exalt the Crown to the possession of all those prerogatives at which Charles the First aimed', while the Whigs sought 'to limit the power of the Crown as much as possible, until prerogative was so much reduced, that the nation should be in fact tho not in form a Republick. The Tories were above all other things fast friends to the House of Stewart: the Whigs fast friends to Liberty alone.' Such a view cannot be accepted without qualification, of course, but it is a reasonable statement of differing attitudes to royal power.

Party battles were very fierce during the reign of Queen Anne (1702–14). Then other aspects of party, which would resurface as important distinguishing features as modern parties developed a century later, came to the fore. Tories were staunch, even fierce, defenders of the Church of England; they opposed the granting of religious toleration to nonconformist dissenters. Whigs supported toleration and, not surprisingly, attracted many dissenters from the expanding middle ranks of society. Throughout the reign, war with France raged. This war, the most costly Britain had yet fought, had to be paid for by taxation and by raising loans for the government. These loans paid useful rates of interest and merchants, traders and contractors benefited substantially from lending money. Those with most money to lend tended to be Whigs and Whigs supported the war. By contrast, smaller landowners increasingly opposed it. English country gentlemen were burdened by a land tax of 20 per cent (four shillings in the pound) levied to help pay for the war. The English counties became increasingly Tory in political sympathy. The land tax hit smaller landowners more heavily than it did commercial men.

By 1714, party allegiance had economic and religious, as well as constitutional dimensions. The Hanoverian succession, however, proved a disaster to the Tory party. The Whigs, always more enthusiastic for a securely Protestant, if German, succession, could soon accuse the Tories of disloyalty, and even treason, towards the new dynasty. Certain Tories were heavily implicated in attempts made in 1715 and 1722 to reimpose a Stuart Catholic dynasty by force. Sir Robert Walpole and other leading Whigs in the 1720s made a most effective job of tarring all Tories with the Jacobite brush, and the Whigs consolidated their control of all the levers of power. Party conflict gave way to rivalry between various Whig groups. Toryism was not destroyed in 1714. As recent research has revealed, it remained an important force in many English counties and some large boroughs. The hundred or so identifiable Tories in parliament by the 1740s, however, had to reconcile themselves to permanent opposition. They combined from time to time with eclipsed, discontented or out-of-favour Whigs to provide criticism of the dominant cliques. The struggle for supremacy in parliament was not between Whig and Tory for almost a century after 1714; it was between Whig and Whig.

With the recession of Whig–Tory rivalry the focus of political debate changed. The crucial element in the second half of the eighteenth century became the role of the monarch. George III's reassertion of independent authority implied an attack on party as a device for limiting his powers. Royal propaganda, therefore, sought to discredit party. In such circumstances, it is not surprising that the revival of that institution was fostered by Whig politicians anxious to vindicate party's legitimate role in the constitution. The Rockingham Whigs, mostly out of office after the 1760s, whereas their predecessors had monopolized it since the 1720s, found in the Dublin lawyer Edmund Burke both a superb political propagandist and a substantial political theorist. His famous pamphlet, *Thoughts on the Causes of the Present Discontents*, published in 1770, offered a cogent defence of party as an institution:

> Party is a body of men united for promoting by their joint endeavours the national interest, upon some particular principle in which they are all agreed. . . . It is the business of the speculative philosopher to mark the proper ends of government. It is the business of the politician, who is the philosopher in action, to find out proper means towards those ends and to employ them with effect. Therefore every honourable connexion will avow it is their first purpose, to pursue every just method to put the men who hold their opinions into such a condition as may enable them to carry their common plans into execution. . . . Such a generous contention for power, on such manly and honourable maxims, will easily be distinguished from the mean and interested struggle for place and emolument.

Party was thus elevated above mere faction, and Whig propaganda asserted that the king had discreditably conflated and confused the two. An early democrat, Capel Lofft, spelled out the distinction in 1779. He believed that faction consisted of 'narrow views, selfish interests, and corrupt measures' whereas party was 'formed for the general good' to promote 'truth, freedom, virtue'.

The king's attack on 'party-men' produced a reaction opposite from that intended. It is one of the more noteworthy features of the period 1784–90 that the opposition did not fragment. On some major issues a cohesive opposition minority of between 120 and 140 could be mustered in the Commons. Much organizational expertise was deployed by William Adam who has some claim to be considered the first professional party manager. He raised funds, helped to select candidates and got them placed in over eighty constituencies. The opposition Whigs appreciated the growing importance of public opinion and Whig funds were given to support both London newspapers like the *Morning Chronicle* and sections of the provincial press. At Westminster, Adam sent notes requesting supporters' attendance for important divisions. The modern system of parliamentary 'whips' was in process of development.

By the end of the 1780s, the term 'leader of the opposition' was coming into use, though applied to Charles James Fox, the active debater in the Commons, rather than to the Duke of Portland, the nominal leader of the old Rockinghams, who sat in the Lords. The personal rivalry of Pitt and Fox helped to sharpen public perceptions of government *versus* opposition in the 1780s. Two other factors are worthy of note. First, opposition continued to cohere on an issue of firm, if misguided, belief: that Pitt was only sustained in office by the illegitimate exercise of royal patronage. Second, when the next general election was held in 1790 the opposition Whigs more or less maintained their voting strength. This may seem unremarkable but it was a substantial achievement nevertheless. Eighteenth-century ministries, once firmly established, almost invariably gained 'converts' from previous opponents now anxious for office. The fact that the Fox–Portland–North opposition Whigs lost few such defectors enabled it to fight the next election in reasonable shape. Thus, a government now in firm control and with substantial achievements to its credit did not reap any particular reward at the hustings.

Pitt might also have expected to do better in 1790 since his Whig opponents had just suffered a major disappointment. In 1788 George III was afflicted with the first of a series of mental disturbances which would eventually remove him from the political scene eight years before his death. After some weeks' illness, there was talk of a Regency headed by the king's eldest son, George, Prince of Wales. 'Prinny', as he was not very affectionately known, was a supporter of the opposition in the manner of most Hanoverian princes-in-waiting who showed their dislike for their fathers by fostering the interests of their opponents. Thus, if a Regency were established nothing was more certain than that the Prince would dismiss Pitt and install Fox in office. Only the king's sudden recovery in February 1789 prevented a change of ministry. During the Regency Crisis the Whigs had made some tactical blunders which Pitt was able to exploit; some disagreements between Fox and Portland were revealed. Nevertheless, the loss of the prospect of office in what must have seemed such arbitrary circumstances would certainly have demoralized an opposition less sure of its ground than Fox's. It was a pro-Pitt commentator, Major John Scott, who analysed the British political system as a two-party one in *Seven Letters to the People of Great Britain*, published in 1789:

> In a free state, and a mixed Government like ours, there will always be two parties; one consisting of the men who compose the Administration, and another consisting of men who want to be in their places . . . as we enjoy the freedom of debate and the liberty of the press, the nation at large is constantly informed of the transactions of Ministers, and of the sentiments of those who oppose them.

Scott was probably jumping his fences before he came to them. Party sentiment in the 1780s was far less developed on the government side.

Like his father, the redoubtable Chatham, Pitt professed a distaste for 'party'. He did less than many eighteenth-century prime ministers to build up a personal following among MPs. He preferred to rely on royal support, on his own mastery of administrative detail which enabled him to control most debates and, increasingly, on financial achievements. These sufficed to keep the independents happy. One estimate of government support in the Commons at the end of the 1780s counts about 185 members whose primary loyalty lay with the king and, through him, to his appointed ministers, 50 or so who attached themselves to Pitt and just over 40 who owed family or patronage allegiance to other ministers, notably Henry Dundas whose control of corrupt Scottish seats was legendary. Pitt took more political concern to strengthen support in the Lords. For a long period during the eighteenth century almost no additions were made to the 200 or so peers. Pitt created over 100 while prime minister, 45 of them between 1784 and 1790. Most became staunch friends of the government in the upper House.

Pitt always called himself a Whig, but he used the term rarely and meant by it little more than one who supported the objectives and achievements of the Glorious Revolution in creating a constitution of balance and mixed powers. Pre-eminently, Pitt was the king's minister, not in the narrow sense of doing the monarch's every bidding, but more broadly. He interpreted his authority as prime minister as deriving from the king's initial choice and subsequent support, and not from any party grouping which happened for the moment to hold a parliamentary majority.

Party issues certainly did not monopolize parliamentary time in the 1780s. The Regency Crisis, which polarized issues very acutely, was out of the routine of business. Part of Pitt's achievement after the 1784 election, indeed, was to lower the temperature of debate in the Commons, just as it was an opposition achievement to preserve the essentials of party identity in a much less favourable climate. It may strike modern readers as odd to learn that the Pitt government was defeated on four substantial issues between 1784 and 1786, including both defence policy and the prime minister's personal proposal to increase county and large town representation at Westminster by removing more than thirty small and 'managed' boroughs from the list of parliamentary seats. On this last question, Pitt found himself in a minority of over seventy. None of these defeats was considered a reason even to contemplate resignation. The British political system was far from the modern practice in which a government presents legislation to the Commons and uses the disciplined (and 'whipped') votes of its supporters to ensure its passage there. Pitt's supporters were an altogether looser and more heterogeneous body, and occasional reverses were considered normal, even on important matters.

Parties and politics in the shadow of the French Revolution, 1788–1812

The French Revolution transformed British political life. Its outbreak shocked the autocratic governments of central and eastern Europe. The prospect of democratic government was not only abhorrent in itself; it would lead to the abandonment of all civilized values. But Britain was not an autocracy. Many experienced political observers here took the patronizing view that, though it had taken the French a century to catch on, their Revolution was a variant of the English Glorious Revolution and would likewise produce a mixed constitution. Even William Pitt anticipated that 'the present convulsions in France must . . . terminate in general harmony and regular order'.

Britain's ruling elite was rapidly to be disabused. In 1792 the French Revolution took a much more radical course. A revolutionary commune was proclaimed in Paris; a republic was declared; armed bands took control of the capital and executed over a thousand political prisoners, many of them landowners and priests; a National Convention was elected on the principle of one man one vote; in January 1793 King Louis XVI was executed; his wife followed him to the guillotine a few months later. These events were assimilated in Britain with horror and disgust by MPs and men of property. Yet, in some ways even more alarming was the establishment in many British towns in 1791 and 1792 of radical associations called Corresponding Societies. These were dedicated to the reform of corrupt government in Britain and the election of a parliament by means of manhood suffrage. The societies, as their name implies, corresponded with one another, held meetings for political discussion and sent messages of support to the French National Convention. Britain was at war with France from February 1793 so such messages were deeply suspect anyway. More worrying to the authorities, however, was the fact that most Corresponding Society members were working men. They represented a new challenge to the existing political system.

Before these developments occurred they had been predicted, in broad outline, by Edmund Burke, the prominent opposition Whig spokesman and writer. In 1790 he published *Reflections on the Revolution in France*. He prophesied that the French Revolution would engender bloodshed, chaos and anarchy since the 'levellers' who had seized control 'never equalize . . . they can only pervert the natural order of things'. Englishmen must awaken to the true nature of the threat, not only in France but within their own country.

Burke's book was more than a first-rate polemic against the Revolution. In attacking that revolution's philosophical basis, he also laid down principles subsequently identified as central to the ideology, not of Whiggery, but of modern Conservatism. French revolutionaries and their sympathizers in Britain based their arguments for change on the principle that men are born with inalienable natural rights. These rights it was the prime task of government to safeguard. It followed logically that, if such rights existed, their most basic expression lay in the right of citizens to choose their governors by democratic process. Burke challenged the notion of equal natural rights. Governments did not derive their authority from the explicit consent of the governed, still less from any implicit 'social contract'. Authority, for Burke, derived from custom, practice and experience. No state could turn its back on the lessons of the past without risking the breakdown of the social order. The prime duty of government, in Burke's eyes, was the preservation of social order. Reliance on speculative theories, however rationally grounded, was no basis for effective or stable government.

Burke was not a reactionary. He argued that a state which did not permit change was a state which had lost the means of conserving itself. He was proud of his Whig reformist origins and remained a believer in equal political rights for Roman Catholics. But, in the fevered climate of the 1790s, Burke stood little chance of being remembered for religious egalitarianism. He gave propertied Englishmen the philosophical and practical armoury with which to fight those detested 'French principles'.

From 1792 onwards, as extra-parliamentary radicalism grew, the vast majority of Englishmen with property of any kind to safeguard rallied to the defence of the existing system. Property was urged as the basis both of the wealth and the stability of the country. Those with property to conserve could be trusted to use their votes and influence wisely, while those without it would be swayed by emotional appeals. The poor were insufficiently educated or reflective to be trusted with votes. If they had them, they would be the dupes of designing 'Jacobins and Atheists' who had imbibed 'French principles'. The outbreak of war with France provided additional patriotic reasons for the defence of things as they were and for the need to repel Jacobinism.

Burke's writings led to a split among the opposition Whigs. Fox broke with Burke in an emotional and tearful scene in the Commons in April 1791. Burke took very few supporters with him then but the events of the following year widened the rift in the party. In 1792 a group of more radical, and generally younger Whigs led by Charles Grey and Samuel Whitbread and aided by the playwright R. B. Sheridan, who had been extravagant in his praise of the Revolution from the beginning, formed an Association of the Friends of the People. It advocated parliamentary reform. These reformers argued that Whiggery implied love of liberty and that parliamentary reform was as clearly in the Whig tradition as was commitment to removing political disabilities from nonconformists. A campaign on this religious issue had received substantial opposition support when debated in the Commons in 1787, 1789 and 1790. It was also in the Whig tradition, the 'radical' Whigs believed, for gentlemen of means to put themselves at the head of various reforming movements which attracted wider support further down the social hierarchy. Now the Whigs were merely asserting 'traditional' controls over a growing extra-parliamentary movement and, in doing so, were seeking to neutralize any wilder excesses. Fox was acutely embarrassed. He was broadly in sympathy with the aims of the Friends of the People, but he knew that they would place the opposition under intolerable strain. His party was now being forced to make an uncomfortable and divisive choice: did it emphasize liberty and reform or order and public security?

One prominent Whig, William Windham, MP for Norwich, where many skilled weavers were ardently embracing 'French principles', answered this question bluntly. He acknowledged that the objectives of the Friends of the People 'may possibly in a very moderate degree be desirable rather than not'. Nevertheless, parliamentary reform was now supported by 'those who mean nothing short of a Complete overthrow of the present Constitution'. Britain was 'a nation great & happy . . . raised to a degree of splendor that has made us the admiration of the World'. To accept reform at this time would 'put all these blessings to Hazard & risk falling into Universal Confusion'. Early in 1793, Windham distanced himself from his leaders and formed a third party of about thirty conservative Whigs who put the defence of the constitution above all else.

Pitt's government was less alarmed at the dangers of extra-parliamentary radicalism than were many opposition Whigs. Between 1792 and 1794 government actions smack of firmness rather than panic. It suited Pitt's book, however, to emphasize the threat to the constitution. In January 1793 this line, and the offer of the Lord Chancellorship, brought over Lord Loughborough from the opposition to the government. For the next eighteen months Fox and Portland strove to keep their party together, but in vain. Fox, against his earlier better judgement, slid ever closer to the reformist Whigs; Portland shared the fears of Windham. When Pitt issued a government proclamation in December 1792 summoning the militia to help defend the country against prospective insurrection, Fox attacked the move as a trick to enable Englishmen's liberties to be curtailed; Portland took the threat seriously. Fox opposed the outbreak of war; Portland regarded it as a regrettable necessity and supported it even after it became clear that it would not quickly be won. Fox supported parliamentary reform when the matter was debated on Grey's motion in the Commons in May 1793; Portland remained resolutely opposed. By the middle of the year, it was clear that opposition unity, so painstakingly preserved during the 1780s, could not survive.

The realignment of political forces which took place in July 1794 was the logical culmination of these developments. Portland accepted high office – the home secretaryship – under Pitt; four other conservative Whigs, Fitzwilliam, Mansfield, Spencer and Windham, entered the Cabinet. The new coalition was a true partnership. Six of the thirteen Cabinet ministers had been anti-Pittites at least before 1793; seven were old associates of the prime minister. Pitt saw the coalition as a working partnership of propertied Britons firm in their resolve to stamp out the heresies of 'Jacobinism, Atheism and Democracy'. He did not see it as a new party, preferring to maintain the view that he was the king's minister presiding over an administration of right-thinking men governing in the national interest. Yet many historians have seen in the formation of the coalition of 1794 the rebirth of the Tory party and the origins of modern Conservatism. Later developments support at least the first of these claims. Pitt may not have been a 'party man', but his new allies certainly were. Moreover, the old conservative Whigs did more than the Pittites to emphasize the anti-reformist nature of new Toryism after 1794. They were more fearful for their property and privileges than was the Pitt group, which consisted increasingly of young men appointed by the prime minister for their administrative and executive talents.

After 1794 what we may call 'new Toryism', though Pitt did not, developed as a party of order which placed social stability, the preservation of the constitution and defence of property above individual liberty and far above either religious or political reform. It was also a party of patriotism, playing on the substantial jingoistic element in British society. Pitt, the parliamentary reformer of 1785, had become its most steadfast opponent by 1797. In his speech against Grey's motion for reform he skilfully blended both order and jingoism, lambasting those 'who hold doctrines which go to the extinction of every branch of the constitution', using parliamentary reform:

> as the first step towards the attainment of their own views . . . who have avowedly borrowed their political creed from the monstrous and detestable system of the French Jacobins . . . that proud, shallow and presumptuous philosophy which . . . has carried theoretical absurdity higher than the wild imaginations of the most extravagant visionaries ever conceived, and practical evil to an extent which no age or history has equalled.

Such wilful hyperbole struck a ready chord both inside parliament and out. The rash of loyalist clubs which spread over Britain in 1792–3 had already shown how popular such sentiments were. The Pittite coalition after 1794 turned conservative sentiment into massive pro-government majorities when the reformers' activities were attacked in 1795. The Seditious Meetings Bill, drastically curtailing the rights of free assembly, passed the Commons by 214 votes to 42. The Treasonable Practices Bill which extended the definition of treason to the point where, as Fox sardonically remarked, Pitt the reformer of the 1780s would have been liable to prosecution under it, was opposed in the Lords by only five peers.

About eighty members of the old Whig opposition had joined Pitt by the middle of 1794. This left Fox with forty to fifty supporters in the Commons, nearly all of them reformers and 'Friends of the People'. Any immediate prospect of office removed, the Foxites who remained could at least allow themselves the luxury of principled opposition. They felt that their old allies had betrayed not only Whiggery but the balanced constitution. Between 1794 and 1797 the Commons witnessed something like a two-party split, though a grossly unequal one. Even the independents were beginning to take sides, though few would yet acknowledge the permanence of party labels. Most, as men of solid property, supported the Pitt line, but a few took the Foxite view that the government now represented a major threat to British liberties. They supported Fox's call for negotiations with France. They also supported Grey's parliamentary reform motion. On this increasingly divisive issue the Foxites were able to muster 91 supporters, roughly double the Foxite 'party' complement, against 256 on the government side.

In some respects the Foxites anticipated the nineteenth-century Liberal party. Their leaders, like those of the later Liberals, were men of aristocratic lineage and influence. They emphasized the liberties of Englishmen and were committed to moderate reform and religious equality. In other respects their feet remained firmly, even anachronistically, in the eighteenth century. For Fox the real enemy remained, as in the 1770s, a king who challenged British liberties by excessive use of court influence. Fox even saw Pitt as a creature of the court. In training his fire so resolutely on the royal target, Fox failed to discern the full significance of extra-parliamentary radicalism and its pointers for the future.

The seductive symmetry of Pitt *v.* Fox, with its attendant two-party associations, was swiftly distorted. Fox's supporters renounced regular parliamentary attendance after the failure of parliamentary reform in 1797. Pitt wrenched the symmetry further in 1801 when he refused to accept a royal veto on the Catholic question (see p. 23) and resigned. What succeeded Pitt suggests confusion. Between 1801 and 1812 seven governments ruled Britain. None, between the long administrations of Pitt (1783–1801) and Liverpool (1812–27), lasted longer than three-and-a-quarter years. The large governing coalition of Pitt was split by his resignation. Even Pitt's personal protégés, cultivated with special emphasis on their administrative competence, disagreed with one another, sometimes violently. Castlereagh and Canning fought a famous duel on Putney Heath in 1809.

When Henry Addington formed his administration in 1801, most Pittites stayed, with the approval of their leader, though Canning not only refused to serve but mounted bitter and wounding personal attacks on the new prime minister. Addington, acutely conscious of his own inexperience and shortcomings (he had previously risen no higher than speaker of the Commons), had made it a condition of accepting office that Pitt would not oppose him. This Pitt readily agreed to, heaping fulsome praise on those of his followers who agreed to serve the new man. Lord Hawkesbury (who became Earl of Liverpool in 1808) was described to the Commons by Pitt as a man to whom none was 'superior . . . in capacity for business'. Pitt doubtless felt that Hawkesbury's rapid elevation to the senior position of foreign secretary from relative obscurity under himself required some special pleading. The Addington administration also divided the conservative Whigs. Of those who had joined Pitt in 1794, Portland stayed in office while Windham and Spencer left.

News of the change of government revived the Foxites. Fox re-appeared in Westminster and garnered 105 votes in an early division against Addington, more than twice the Foxite strength in the mid-1790s. Further grounds for optimism were discovered in 1802 when Lord Grenville, who had been a Pittite minister continuously from 1789 to 1801, went into open opposition in disgust at Addington's peace terms during a brief lull in the French wars. Grenville and Windham formed a separate war party of about thirty. They included many senior men, were good debaters and offered the prospect of eventual alliance with the Whigs.

Addington's administration slithered ignominiously towards its end after the wars resumed. Faced with the prime minister's manifest incompetence, Pitt's benevolent neutrality could no longer be guaranteed and when Addington eventually resigned in 1804, Pitt himself was the obvious replacement. George III overlooked the reason for his requiring Pitt's resignation in 1801 in the face of a greater and more immediate threat from Napoleon. Pitt retained his popularity with the country gentlemen and could command a parliamentary majority.

Pitt's second administration, however, was far weaker than his first. He could not even bring all of his old personal following back. George Canning would not serve with Castlereagh and preferred to exercise his waspish debating talents against his old colleagues; in the process, he came increasingly within the orbit of Grenville. Grenville would only serve if Fox, now in favour of war since Napoleon declared himself Emperor, could be brought into government in a grand coalition to wage war, and to this the king would not agree. The developing Fox–Grenville alliance presented formidable opposition to Pitt, though personal jealousies played at least as great a part as did party sympathy in determining alliances. Contemporaries discerned four political groupings around the leading personalities of Pitt in office, and Fox, Grenville and Addington out of it. It was not the basis for stability.

The Pitt government might well have collapsed anyway, but the great man's premature death in January 1806 threw matters into further confusion, precipitating the last political crisis in which the monarch played the decisive part. Most loyal Pittites preferred to resign immediately upon their mentor's death, and looked forward to a beneficial period of regrouping and revival in opposition. Aristocratic politicians of the early nineteenth century, it might be remarked, viewed the loss of office with considerably greater equanimity than do their less aristocratic twentieth-century successors. This is partly because loss of office nowadays implies rejection by the electorate and such rejection is always wounding if not humiliating. Nineteenth-century politics, however, was a less full-time and professional affair, and the aristocratic life-style was almost bound to offer attractive alternatives to running a department of state.

In the event, their brief period out of office in 1806–7 brought the Pittites closer together as a group. Hawkesbury's and Castlereagh's resignations left George III with as few alternatives as he had had in 1783. Now, as then, Fox must come back into office if there was to be a government at all. Now, as then, the king had him on sufferance. The new government, headed by Grenville with Fox as foreign secretary, laboured under the heavy disability of royal resentment. Grenville's attempt to forge a coalition, widely but mistakenly dubbed the 'Ministry of all the Talents', worked so far only as to include Addington (ennobled as Viscount Sidmouth in 1805) and his circle. The most 'talented' parliamentary elements, in fact, were the Pittites who stayed out. From 1806 the Pittites began to operate as a party in a way of which Pitt himself would never have approved.

The Talents were a Whig-dominated coalition though, with Grenville at the helm, never so reformist as the old Foxites. No action was taken on the most important tenets of Whig reformist faith, religious concessions in Ireland and parliamentary reform. Both were offensive to the Addingtonians. Fox's death in November removed the Talents' most eminent member and a general election held at the end of the year showed no evidence of great popular support for the government. George was emboldened to be rid of an administration unpopular both with himself and, apparently, the nation. The fact that the war was going badly did not help Grenville either. Wrangling split the ministry; Sidmouth resigned in March 1807; George removed the remaining ministers a week later. Most Whigs would not see office again until 1830.

The spring of 1807 marks an important stage in the history of party politics. George III could turn to a rejuvenated Pittite group, though he looked to the far from rejuvenated – indeed increasingly decrepit – Duke of Portland to provide seniority as prime minister. The new ministry included both Castlereagh (war office) and Canning (foreign secretary), while Hawkesbury returned to the home office. These three, though they differed in almost every personal respect, were the ablest torchbearers of the Pittite tradition and the Pittites were now in the process of making themselves the basis of a Tory party. The chancellor of the exchequer was Spencer Perceval, a conscientious and sober man from the Addington group who had recently abandoned the law for a full-time career in politics. Sidmouth himself stayed out. As in 1784, George III held an early general election to confirm his ministry in power. As in 1784, it worked. In the election of 1807, 138 MPs were defending seats first won in the election of the previous year. Ninety-five of these were considered supporters of the Talents and 43 against them; 49 of the former group lost their seats in 1807 and only 10 of the latter. The new government achieved this success despite the nationwide circulation of political propaganda by the Whig opposition. This direct appeal to the electorate itself emphasized the growing importance of general elections.

The development of Toryism between 1807 and 1812, however, was anything but smooth. Once again, personal rivalries determined political allegiance and the final mental collapse of George III was a further obstacle to stable government. Dominating everything was the progress of the war and the increased taxation and commercial difficulties to which its long continuance was giving rise. Ministries had to contend with the revival of extra-parliamentary criticism and opposition.

Illness finally forced Portland's retirement in 1809. His successor, Perceval, could not keep the increasingly self-regarding Pittites together. Characteristically, Canning would not serve under a man he considered his junior both in experience and abilities. Castlereagh also went. Nevertheless, it remained possible to describe the new government as Tory: it was the king's choice and his ministers supported royal authority; it was opposed to Catholic emancipation; it opposed reform. In the face of able attacks from Canning and his friends, however, Perceval felt that he needed to broaden the base of his administration. Initial overtures to Grey and Grenville were rebuffed and the Whig opposition harboured expectations in 1810–11 that the advent of the Prince Regent would bring a change in their fortunes more attractive than any prospect of serving under Spencer Perceval. Not until March 1812 did the government look secure, when its anti-reformist base was strengthened by the return of the important figures of Sidmouth and Castlereagh. And then, his ministry apparently well secured, Perceval was shot dead in the lobby of the House of Commons by a bitterly resentful and probably deranged bankrupt, John Bellingham. Spencer Perceval thus entered the large print of historical reputation not as the man who consolidated the Tory party (as well he might have done, given the conditions which Liverpool would inherit), but as the only British prime minister so far to have been assassinated.

Lord Liverpool succeeded Perceval and, given both the eventual length of his administration and the prime minister's later indispensability, one might assume that the regent's choice was obvious. Not so. The regent offered the prime ministership to no less than five candidates in the spring of 1812 before it was given to Liverpool. This apparent slight to a man who then settled in to become the third longest serving premier in history is easily explained. Liverpool was not senior enough or brilliant enough to compel selection as the obvious Pittite. The appointment of Perceval in 1809 and in not dissimilar circumstances had given George III considerable trouble. The regent calculated that it would be better to try, yet again, for a broad-based coalition. His failure supports the contention that party consciousness was growing. The Whig opposition much preferred government on their own and believed that they deserved the opportunity to succeed where the Talents had failed.

The government which Liverpool eventually formed was very similar to that of Perceval in his last weeks. It remained strongly anti-reformist and included, in Sidmouth, Castlereagh and the Lord Chancellor, Eldon, men of experience and weight. Opposed to them, yet again, was Canning, both an ex-Pittite and a strong opponent of political reform but, significantly, in favour of relief to the Catholics. Grey and Grenville, political opponents in the 1790s, were now widely recognized as close allies in the opposition Whig interest. Grenville's presence was important to the Whigs in these years. He contributed to the increasing wariness with which senior Whigs approached the reform question. The party included men, like Francis Burdett, who remained ardent reformers, but they were not in senior positions and the Whigs after Fox were less inclined to emphasize their links with extra-parliamentary radicalism. One leading Whig aristocrat, Lord Holland, declared roundly in 1816: 'The nearer I look to parliamentary reform the less I own I like it.' The key to such Whig solidarity as existed at this time remained the increasingly anachronistic urge to curb the influence of the crown. Whether their leaders welcomed it or not, however, the Whigs were receiving increasing support from hard-pressed industrialists and commercial men in the north of England, where the early stages of the industrial revolution were providing at least as much crisis as opportunity while the war dragged on. The links between the Whig party and commerce had been important before (see p. 8), and would be crucial in the years ahead. In 1812 the selection of Liverpool, a strong pro-war man and secretary for war under Perceval, provoked riots in Lancashire.

The decline of royal influence, 1780–1840

The Whig opposition continued to believe, at least until about 1820, that its main enemy was the crown. This understandable eighteenth-century reaction was increasingly inappropriate. The powers of the monarchy declined quite rapidly in this period, with profound implications for the clarity of party divisions. Much of the politics of the later eighteenth century could be characterized as a struggle between the king and his friends on the one hand and landowning politicians

21

zealous to maintain the privileges of parliament on the other. Once this characterization no longer held, the focus of debate had to change. The opposition Whigs recognized very late that their opponents were not simple court lackeys and they paid the price for their slowness of perception in the inordinately long period out of government which they had to endure before 1830.

Royal power had rested on the ability to appoint men to household, revenue and other administrative posts. Many of these were either peers of the realm or commoners who could be selected to represent those small boroughs in the House of Commons which were under the control of the king. This system of political patronage has been briefly outlined elsewhere (12). The king's influence, especially in the House of Lords, was very strong in the later eighteenth century. In the early 1780s, thirty peers holding royal appointments sat in the Lords. In a chamber containing little more than two hundred members, many of whom were infrequent attenders, such a loyal and acting voting element was frequently decisive.

Opposition politicians naturally sought to curb such royal influence. The temporary triumph of the 'politicians' in 1782 produced three Acts with this objective. Burke's Act abolished a number of government and court sinecure appointments and subjected the Civil List (royal income voted by parliament) to much closer scrutiny. Crewe's Act prohibited nominated revenue officers from becoming MPs, and Clerk's Act did the same for government contractors. This legislation had far less significance, however, than the reforms of the younger Pitt. His quest was not to curb royal power but to reduce government debt and increase administrative efficiency. The recent War of American Independence had proved very costly and Pitt saw in the reduction of sinecures a means of lessening government expenditure. Pitt's adviser, George Pretyman, estimated that more than 400 revenue posts were abolished between 1783 and 1793. The move to match posts to duties rather than influence continued after Pitt's death though, naturally, at greater speed during stable ministries than unstable ones. More than 2000 sinecure offices were abolished between 1815 and 1822. By 1819, Lord Liverpool's patronage secretary, Charles Arbuthnot, was noting, with unconscious irony in his use of the word 'independent': 'With all our sweeping reductions of patronage I have not the tie I once had upon the independent members.'

Patronage was usually placed at the disposal of ministers who retained royal confidence. These reforms meant, however, that the monarch could no longer use such influence either to bolster a newly installed government or to act against one he wished to remove. As we have seen, the king used patronage in the House of Lords to unseat the Fox–North coalition in 1783. George III was able to exercise considerable powers thereafter, though partly because of his experience and the respect in which he was held by most politicians outside the Foxite circle. His determination to prohibit Catholic emancipation in Ireland ensured Pitt's resignation in 1801, though the prime minister had a huge majority in the Commons. Royal disapproval emphasized the impermanence of the Talents ministry in 1806 and royal influence helped to strengthen the Portland ministry which followed it (see pp. 19–20). Royal influence, though waning, still mattered.

The real effects of declining royal influence did not become brutally apparent until the reigns of George III's sons, George IV (1820–30) and William IV (1830–37). By the end of George IV's reign 'political' court patronage was almost a thing of the past. The House of Lords, increased to about 400 members since the early 1780s, now contained only 18 peers who held household appointments and might be expected to support the king through thick and thin. The Duke of Wellington, who sat there as prime minister between 1828 and 1830, impotently admitted just before he left office: 'No government can go on without some means of rewarding services. I have absolutely none.' What he meant was that the only basis for government, even before the passage of the first Reform Act in 1832, was a secure Commons majority. It was significant that at the general election of 1830, made necessary by the death of George IV, Wellington lost support despite the known preference of the new king, a naval man, for Wellington, a military man of the highest standing. In the 1830 elections some loyal government supporters who were opposed to reform lost their seats in constituencies where public opinion mattered.

In the autumn of 1834 William IV, quite unjustifiably fearful of the extent of radical influence within the Whig government then headed by Viscount Melbourne, used his royal prerogative to dismiss his ministers despite the fact that they had a secure majority. He appointed a Tory government in its stead. So unexpected and quixotic was the king's behaviour, a botched attempt to repeat the circumstances of 1783–4, in fact, that the new prime minister, Sir Robert Peel, had to rush back from Italy to receive the seals of office. The minority Tory government was then, like Pitt's in 1784, given a general election – again at royal instigation – in an attempt to secure a majority. Though the Tories did make gains, they were not sufficient and it was extremely doubtful if any could be attributed to the enlarged electorate's desire to follow their king's political preferences. The Whigs and their allies had a majority of over one hundred and Peel was forced to resign a few weeks after the election. For the first time, a Hanoverian monarch had failed to 'make' a new ministry by the use of an election. Never again would a monarch dismiss a ministry which retained Commons support. Only rarely would royal preferences be of much significance in the choice of ministers. While independent royal influence was effectively at an end, general elections became ever more important.

With crown patronage and influence drastically diminished, an important source of authority disappeared. Party developed still further, in part to fill the power vacuum. The younger Pitt could plausibly assert that he was not a party man and refuse to organize his followers into a party. The same luxury was not open to Lord Liverpool in the 1810s and 1820s. Though many of Liverpool's Pittites might express distaste at the notion of party and profess that their first loyalty was to the monarch, they could not keep themselves in office without party organization. The long Liverpool administration was the first stable government which needed to give as much attention to party groupings and political organization as the opposition had been doing since the days of Burke and the Rockingham Whigs in the early 1780s.

It is also possible to discern the growth of Cabinet identification, and even solidarity, as a partial consequence of declining royal power. Senior ministers, knowing that access to the royal closet was now of limited value to their political careers, established their positions by more collective action and, where necessary and in exceptional circumstances, by threat of collective resignation. In 1821, Liverpool tried hard to obtain Canning's readmittance to the government against great hostility from the king, who loathed Canning and suspected him of having been his wife's lover (or, more accurately, one of her many lovers). The king's will was temporarily the stronger, since Liverpool was not prepared to resign on the issue. When Castlereagh committed suicide the following year, however, the government took the view that Canning was the only possible replacement as foreign secretary. Liverpool canvassed ministers of all opinions and, when he was assured that even those most unsympathetic to Canning saw no alternative to him, presented the king with what amounted to an ultimatum to appoint him. The king backed down with that ill grace and vituperation which his ministers knew well. Canning's appointment was, he said, 'the greatest sacrifice of my opinions and feelings that I have ever made in my life'. Constitutionally, the important point was that he still made it.

In 1823, on a less memorable issue, Liverpool further demonstrated the superior power of Cabinet judgement over royal preference. George IV had wanted to make his private secretary a privy councillor. When the government objected, the king threatened to dismiss Liverpool. The prime minister, a mild, even dull man to whom flamboyant utterance was completely alien, nevertheless brutally reminded his monarch of the new facts of political life. George would find no replacement remotely palatable to him, or able to command a Commons majority: 'The King will find himself very much mistaken if he supposes that if he dismissed me . . . Canning or Peel or any of my colleagues would remain behind.'

The decline of the monarchy was also hastened by personal factors. George III's influence was weakened by recurrent mental instability after 1788, and he ceased to function at all after 1810. The Prince Regent inspired almost no respect in political circles, being reputed vindictive and licentious, lazy, unpredictable and lacking in judgement. He was precisely the wrong man to shore up monarchical influence at a time when its direct power was waning. Liverpool's ministers learned that they could brave his fits of temper and outbursts of outrageousness with very little loss to themselves. George's brother, William IV, was a distinct improvement in personal terms, but little trained in political management and disastrously inept. By the time that Queen Victoria came to the throne in 1837, a totally inexperienced and rather empty young woman of eighteen, her famous, even touching, reliance on her prime minister, Lord Melbourne, was rather a political hindrance than a help to her ministers. Victoria's Prince Consort, Albert of Saxe–Coburg–Gotha, would need all his sterling qualities of heavy, teutonic endeavour to restore the monarchy in the 1840s and 1850s to prestige and dignified reputation, if not direct power.

Stability, religion and reform, 1812–32

The only hindrance to the open acknowledgement of Lord Liverpool's government as a Tory administration was historical. For some, 'Tory' still implied opposition, if not disloyalty. A ministerial memorandum to the Prince Regent in 1812 reflected this sentiment:

> It is almost unnecessary to observe that the British government . . . could only be a Whig government; and that the present administration is a Whig administration. For a Whig government means as it has all along meant nothing else than a government established by laws equally binding upon the King and the Subject.

Few believed this any longer. By the end of the decade it was universally held that Liverpool's was a Tory government which was faced in the Commons by a smaller, but still reasonably cohesive, Whig opposition. In the absence of a disciplined system of whips, and with variable attendance, precise figures of support for the parties are impossible, but the estimates of Austin Mitchell strongly suggest that a kind of two-party system was operating at Westminster (7). In the parliament of 1812–18, 253 firm government (Tory) supporters have been identified, with 149 equally firm opposition (Whig) supporters against them. To these might be added a further 78 'waverers' who usually supported the government and 83 opposition-inclined waverers. This left only 102 members out of 665 whose party views were not broadly identifiable; some of these still prided themselves on solid 'independence' of view. Figures for the early 1820s show a similar pattern. Support for government, opposition and 'independent', expressed in ratio terms, stood at 7:4:2 respectively. It is noteworthy that the Whigs, though in a minority in the Commons as a whole, were in a very substantial majority among that small but important group of MPs elected from the large boroughs and more populous counties where public opinion had an effective electoral voice.

Liverpool's government, therefore, was not fully secure against a combined assault from Whigs and independents. Only a few issues were likely to bring such a challenge, however, and one was taxation. It is not surprising that a defeat, rare but significant, came in 1816 on Liverpool's proposal to retain the lucrative and efficient income tax in peacetime. Even some 'government waverers' marched into the opposition lobby on this sensitive question and the government lost by 40 votes. The reintroduction of income tax was delayed for a generation until Peel had the determination to push the measure through in 1842, but only immediately after a decisive general election victory and when party discipline had become tighter.

The social background of MPs supporting the two party groupings reveals interesting variations. Between 50 and 60 per cent of both Tory and Whig MPs were either themselves, or were closely related to, large landowners. Among MPs with a commercial background, however, roughly twice as many Whigs were found as Tories. The Tories had a roughly equivalent advantage in the not unimportant category of retired army and navy officers. In some respects, as we shall see, differences in social composition were more marked between the parties than were differences in policy.

Stability is the keynote of Liverpool's long administration and it is worth enquiring why, after a decade of profound instability, his government was able to survive for almost fifteen years. Luck undoubtedly played its part early on. The general election of 1812 did not strengthen the ministry's position much. Before ministries were fully established the possibility of counter-groupings always existed and adverse votes, especially in the Commons, could be damaging. Liverpool was helped through this bumpy early period by the fact that national attention was concentrated on the war with France and that, finally, the war was being won. The Duke of Wellington's hard slog in the Peninsula and Napoleon's crucial decision to invade Russia thus both helped to secure Liverpool's position. Furthermore, the Grey–Grenville opposition was split over the war, the Grenvillites urging vigorous endeavours while the Grey element argued during 1813 for immediate peace. Liverpool was thus allowed the luxury of an opposition divided on the crucial issue of the day. The strong conservative coalition of Pittites and Addingtonians was firmly in the saddle by the end of 1815, under a prime minister whose reputation as the most senior and experienced of the old Pittites made him a natural choice as leader.

Until recently, Liverpool's reputation among historians stood low. Disraeli's later description of him as the 'arch mediocrity' has stuck. Recent rehabilitations, notably by Norman Gash (19), have gone too far in the opposite direction, but no man retains power at the highest level for as long as Liverpool without some bankable assets. Liverpool's abilities were of the undemonstrative kind, which is doubtless why they were lost on Disraeli whose own political judgements were usually based upon meretricious criteria. Liverpool did not have an original mind; he was no innovator; but his talents contributed to his administration's stability. He was a man with whom others could work, a considerate yet shrewd chairman of Cabinet, a good speaker in the House of Lords and an efficient, conscientious administrator. He was, assuredly, dull but in the climate of the times even this may have been an advantage. The press in the 1810s was playing a large part in moulding public opinion and public opinion itself was growing in importance. The widespread distress of the period 1815–20 was a godsend to polemical journalists and cartoonists. Men's reputations could be jeopardized, it sometimes seemed, almost by a stroke of the pen. The Prince Regent's unattractive personality was brought vividly and persistently to public notice and undoubtedly helped to reduce the status of the monarchy. Liverpool's government was viciously criticized, especially in the radical press. The fact that the prime minister's private life was blameless and his reputation for hard work unimpeachable deprived his opponents of some of the most damaging weapons in the political arsenal.

Once established under a competent prime minister, an administration before 1832 could usually count on important accessions of support, at least from those for whom the prospect of long-term opposition was unalluring. George Canning was brought into the administration in 1816. His oratorical talents were much needed since Liverpool, who sat in the Lords, lacked good speakers in the lower House and possessed, in Nicholas Vansittart, one of the most spectacularly inarticulate chancellors of the exchequer of the nineteenth century. In 1818 the Duke of Wellington accepted a ministerial post. Wellington was no politician, and was to prove the point with two unhappy years as prime minister from 1828 to 1830, but he had great national prestige as the victor of Waterloo and he gave the government additional authority. The fact that a non-party man like Wellington should take Tory colours to become a minister indicates the growing acceptability of party government.

The most satisfying new support came from the Grenvillites. Relations between the Foxites and the Grenville clan grew more distant after 1815, and became especially strained over questions of public order when the parliamentary reform question revived under the stimulus of economic depression. Grenville, whose warm personal regard for Grey had always been an important factor in the alliance, took a less active part in politics while his successor as leader of the group, the Duke of Buckingham, hated Foxite Whiggery. After 1818, the Grenville group separated from the opposition and worked for a time as a small, personal, third party. In 1822 they openly declared their support for Liverpool and their Commons spokesman, Charles Wynn, accepted a Cabinet post. The Whigs were reduced to something like their old Foxite base. Grey, as he had done in 1797, again withdrew temporarily from the political stage, mournfully reflecting in 1824 that 'there is no public question which excites . . . no public prospects which can engage one in future speculations'.

The economic and political instability of the period 1815–20, perhaps paradoxically, also helped to strengthen Liverpool's parliamentary position. The revival of extra-parliamentary agitation sent shivers up propertied spines. For many politicians, 1815–20 was the 1790s writ large; their reaction was similar. They rallied behind a government which declared its priority to be the preservation of public order. The government's temporary suspension of Habeas Corpus in 1817 and the 'Six Acts' of 1819, which included the prohibition of mass meetings and the regulation of newspapers, were massively unpopular in the towns but they passed easily through both Houses of Parliament. Independents and Grenvillites showed their support for the administration's determination to defend property. Even among the Whigs, attacks on the government's legislation were often muted. Parliamentary reform was not an issue around which the party could confidently rally. Splits

28

were revealed between radical Whigs and more cautious figures who, by 1819, certainly included Grey himself. The Whig party in the Commons was very difficult to lead. George Ponsonby, who did the job from 1807 to his death in 1817, had few talents beyond his ability to conciliate. His successor, George Tierney (1818–21), was a decided improvement but was selected largely because he would not antagonize moderate elements within the party as would the more prominent radical contenders, Samuel Romilly and Henry Brougham. Whig weaknesses and uncertainties in the Commons counterbalanced the Liverpool government's relative lack of debating talent there before 1822.

It has often been asserted that the Liverpool government falls naturally into two phases: a 'reactionary' one from 1812–22, characterized by legislation to suppress liberties and defend public order and symbolized by anti-reforming ministers such as Eldon and Castlereagh; and a 'liberal' one from 1822–7, characterized by reforms in trade, financial policy and the legal system and symbolized by 'liberal Tories' like Huskisson and Robinson. The distinction is too crude and derives from excessive concentration on the personalities, rather than the policies, of the Liverpool government. Liverpool's 'new men' – Huskisson, Robinson and Peel – had been valued members of his government for several years before 1822, though in more minor positions. They were all able and had deserved promotion. Sidmouth and Vansittart, who both accepted less senior government posts, were 65 and 56 respectively in 1822; their successors, Peel and Robinson, were 34 and 40. These two, and the rather older William Huskisson, were imbued with the reforming vitality which is the hallmark of able politicians on the way up. The policies they were putting into effect, however, had been substantially agreed by their predecessors and always with the concurrence of Liverpool himself. The general economic strategy was determined in 1819–20. It was to stimulate national revival by a policy of sound money and giving a stimulus to trade. Indirect taxes were to be reduced and interest rates to fall. Liverpool's own Pittite background could be discerned here. As early as 1812 he had stated that 'the less commerce and manufactures were meddled with the more likely they were to prosper'. Frederick Robinson's budget of 1824, which reduced excise duties, had been approved in outline by Vansittart. Some of Peel's legal reforms had been proposed in the time of Sidmouth. Even in foreign policy it is now widely agreed that the main difference between Castlereagh, who committed suicide in 1822, and Canning, who replaced him as foreign secretary, was in style not content. Castlereagh would surely have recognized the South American

29

republics, as Canning did, and had already turned his back on what he saw as the reactionary policies of Russia and Austria, Britain's allies in the peacemaking endeavours of 1814–15.

The true difference between the allegedly 'reactionary' and 'liberal' phases of Liverpool's government lies in the state of the economy and the extent of popular unrest to which it gave rise. The French wars had been ruinously expensive. At their end government expenditure totalled £30 million with income of only £12 million. The deficit could not be met by income tax so it was accommodated by further borrowing, savings on expenditure which involved further pruning of patronage appointments (see p. 22), and a heavily deflationary policy. This exacerbated problems of unemployment, since over 300,000 recently demobilized men were already glutting the labour market. Radical protests, which culminated in the 'Peterloo' Massacre of 1819, took place against a background of economic crisis. By contrast, Huskisson, Robinson and Peel had the good fortune to operate in calmer, more expansionist times, with the solitary exception of the period of financial crisis in 1825–6. Extra-parliamentary agitation ebbed markedly after 1821 and the government could afford to give its attention to economic revival rather than public order. Economic policy was not a particularly contentious party issue. Liverpool's policy of trade liberalization followed in the footsteps of Pitt's peacetime administration (1783–93) and within the context of Adam Smith's overall philosophy. To that philosophy most Whig spokesmen warmly subscribed.

The government reshuffle of 1822–3 did have important consequences for religious policy, however. Religion generated far more party heat than did the technicalities of economic theory. It was a 'gut' issue; it stirred both emotions and prejudices; and all politicians could join in. The promotion of Canning and his ally Huskisson, together with the inclusion of the Grenvillites, strengthened that group within the government which favoured increased political liberties for Roman Catholics both in Ireland and Great Britain. The Catholic Emancipation question in the 1820s was given greater point by the emergence of Daniel O'Connell and his Catholic Association in Ireland. But for Liverpool's own authority, which enabled him to declare Catholic relief an 'open question' upon which ministers might legitimately hold opposite views and vote in different ways, the Tories might have impaled themselves on the religious hook earlier than they did. The party was effectively divided between 'Ultras' and 'liberals'. Protestant Ultras like Eldon, Wellington and Peel opposed any concessions to the Catholics. Nevertheless, the support of the Whigs ensured Commons majorities for Canning's bill in 1822 to admit Catholic peers to Parliament and for the Whig Francis Burdett's Catholic Relief Bill in 1825. The 'Protestants' had to rely on their strength in the Lords to defeat both proposals. The Catholic question featured prominently in the otherwise unmemorable general election of 1826 and provided evidence, to be repeated in elections held on a wider franchise after 1832, that the English voting public was much more 'Protestant' than 'liberal' on religion.

Religion had become a persistent sore in the last years of the Liverpool government. When the prime minister had to resign early in 1827, following a serious stroke, the protective covering was removed. The opened wound rapidly festered in the poisonous atmosphere of religious bigotry. The consequences for the Tory party were nearly fatal. Religion and parliamentary reform dominated the turbulent period of five-and-a-half years between Liverpool's resignation and the passage of the first Reform Act.

Liverpool had been one of the few Tory ministers to work amicably with Canning, and it was known that the ambitious and waspish foreign secretary was his chosen successor. George IV's meek acceptance of his former prime minister's preference showed that even the deepest personal antagonisms could be overcome and, perhaps, that the king no longer cared much for politics. Canning's appointment was extremely controversial. Wellington (who loathed him), Eldon and Peel refused to serve under him. The new prime minister seized a fleeting opportunity to fashion an alliance of religious 'liberals' and immediately approached leading Whigs for their support. Tierney, Lansdowne and the Earl of Carlisle accepted the invitation. Grey, disgusted, disowned them publicly. Canning had thus split both parties within two months. His sudden death in August 1827 only made matters worse since his successor, Robinson, now ennobled as Viscount Goderich, inherited the same weakened ministerial team and possessed far fewer talents for leadership than his predecessor. An efficient chancellor of the exchequer, Goderich was painfully aware of his own inadequacies as prime minister and, when George IV demanded his resignation in January 1828, it was a debatable point which of the two men was the more relieved at his departure.

The king's only alternative after the failure of the uneasy alliances of 1827 was a remodelled Tory government with Wellington as prime minister and Robert Peel leading in the Commons. The Tierney–Lansdowne Whigs withdrew but, for a time, the more liberal Tories headed by Huskisson stayed in office. This attempt to rebuild the Tory party as it had been in the last years under Liverpool stood little chance of success. Wellington was little more enamoured of Canning's old supporters, the Huskissonites, than he had been of Canning himself. The prominence of the religious question ensured that 'Protestant' Tories were keen to be rid of them too. Huskisson and his allies left office in May 1828 on a trivial matter which, had the lack of sympathy between ministers not been so profound, would never have been a resignation issue.

Wellington's government thereafter was narrowly based, far weaker in debating talent in the Commons and, perhaps most important, increasingly out of sympathy with public opinion. As economic depression and dislocation returned at the end of the 1820s, reform agitation reached new heights. Peel, who had remarked to a friend in 1820 that public opinion appeared more liberal than the tone of the government, found himself in 1828 a leading minister in a far more narrowly based 'Protestant' administration beset by fundamental economic and political problems.

Those who most welcomed the departure of the Huskissonites were the backbench Ultra Tories. These were hard-line opponents of every kind of reform who believed in the absolute supremacy of the Anglican church and no concessions on any 'liberal' issue. They were particularly strongly represented in the small, 'rotten' parliamentary boroughs and in some of the English counties. Few were practical politicians and they misjudged their men in believing that Wellington and, particularly, Peel were as reactionary as they. They were not pleased when the government repealed the Test and Corporations Acts in 1828, thus permitting Protestant dissenters to hold office. They tolerated it only because the old statutes had become virtual dead letters. Nevertheless, their repeal gave aid and comfort to reformers who began to believe, for the first time since the 1780s, that they might be pushing at an open door.

Catholic Emancipation was a different matter for the Ultras. It was bound up with Ireland, self-determination and nationalism. When the Catholic nationalist politician, Daniel O'Connell, was elected for the Irish seat of County Clare in 1828 he forced the issue since no Catholic could take his seat in the Commons. Peel, who had been chief secretary for Ireland and knew the lie of the land, advised Wellington that failure to grant political concessions to the Irish Catholics would endanger the Union of the kingdoms and quite possibly provoke civil war. With liberal votes in the Commons, Catholic Emancipation was pushed through in 1829, by a Protestant Tory government. The Ultras felt betrayed. A fundamental tenet of Tory belief had been abandoned by their own. Wellington was described by the Duke of Newcastle as 'a most unprincipled . . . and most dangerous man'. Lord Falmouth talked of Catholic Emancipation laying an axe to the root of the very constitution which it was the sacred trust of Tories to uphold.

The Tories were now divided into three feuding fragments: supporters of Wellington and Peel, who staggered on in government until November 1830; the Ultras; and the Huskissonite 'liberals'. Mutual antagonism made it impossible to hold the line against parliamentary reform when that question was raised with increasing urgency outside parliament from 1829 onwards. The story of the agitation for reform has been told in some detail elsewhere (12). Here it is only necessary to note that reform brought Wellington down to be replaced by a Whig government headed by Earl Grey. He took office committed to passing a Reform Act for which all the evidence of the general elections of 1830 and 1831 suggested there was overwhelming extra-parliamentary support. Significantly, Grey included in his government Goderich, Palmerston and Grant, members of the Canning–Huskisson liberal Tory element who had progressed from support for religious reform to accepting the necessity of a widened franchise and the abolition of rotten boroughs.

Peel, demoralized, retired to his Staffordshire country seat of Drayton Manor, there to work off his frustrations by playing at practical farming, a task for which he was ludicrously ill suited. The extent of the Whig proposals, particularly their implications for the removal of Tory seats in rotten boroughs, rallied the opposition somewhat in 1831. But the struggle was hopeless; politics were polarized into pro-reform and anti-reform camps. The anti-reformers were increasingly out of touch with extra-parliamentary reality, however much they might continue to hope that the House of Lords would throw out reform. In 1832 even this hope disappeared and the newly extended electorate was given an early chance to express its views. The first elections for the reformed parliament gave the Whigs and their reforming allies a huge majority; the Tories were reduced to a rump of fewer than 200 MPs. For a natural party of government, which the Tories had become since 1794, it was a profound shock. As Charles Arbuthnot, the party's chief organizer, gloomily indicated: 'No smash given by Napoleon in the midst of his greatest successes was more complete and terrific than the overthrow which has struck our party to the ground.'

The establishment of two-party politics, 1832–46

One historian has argued that 'The essential ingredients of the British two-party system had . . . not only appeared but had been largely accepted both by politicians and by public opinion by 1832' (4). It is a tempting thesis. We have seen ample evidence of politicians at Westminster thinking on increasingly two-party lines after 1794. Though party allegiances were in total confusion, especially on the Tory side, between 1827 and 1832, the polarizing power of religion and parliamentary reform virtually removed the independent MP as a separate factor in Westminster politics. After 1832, almost all politicians adopted party labels when they stood for election. The evident collapse of the power of the crown further reduced the possibilities of alternative allegiance.

We must be cautious about accepting this thesis, however. Party organization and party discipline alike were much increased only after 1832, as we shall see. In the Reform Act crisis itself, furthermore, politicians readily moved between parties. Such movement was much more painful and much more protracted after 1846 (see pp. 45–51). Between 1828 and 1832 the Canningites effectively became Whigs and their most able lieutenant, Viscount Palmerston, was installed as Grey's foreign secretary. Tory party allegiance at the same time became much more fluid. Peel remained in open dispute with the 'Ultras' who made up the bulk of the Tory group after the 1832 election. Gash believes that in 1832 there 'was no acknowledged head and no real party'.

The election of 1832 was not properly between Whigs and Tories. Rather, it was fought between those who supported, and those who had opposed, the principle of parliamentary reform. The former, much larger, category included about fifty moderate reformers who saw the necessity for reform in 1832 to avert revolution but who were firm opponents of radicalism and staunch adherents of the Church of England. At the other pole were about one hundred variegated and disunited radical reformers who included democrats, republicans, free traders and advocates of the disestablishment of the Church of England. In 1832–3 many of these radicals opposed ministerialist reformers, the main props of Grey's government, at least as often as they supported them.

From this confusion a closer two-party alignment than ever was visible by the end of 1835. In June 1834 the Whigs were weakened by the resignation from the Cabinet of two firm Church of England men, Sir James Graham and Lord Stanley, on the divisive issue of 'appropriation'. This entailed drawing off surplus revenue owned by the Anglican church in Ireland and diverting it to non-religious purposes such as educational and social reforms. Appropriation was widely interpreted among moderates and Tories as an attack on the Church. Their feeling of unease was strengthened in July when Grey resigned as prime minister, to be replaced by Melbourne. Melbourne was no radical, but Irish MPs who followed O'Connell and were enthusiastic advocates of appropriation used the change of government to move closer to the Whigs in the hope of pushing the measure through. More MPs began to see why Graham and Stanley had resigned.

These two leading politicians refrained from formally joining the Tories for the remainder of the 1830s. They formed the 'Derby Dilly' (named after the title to which Stanley was heir), a separate group of around forty moderates, increasingly sympathetic to Peel. Graham and Peel became personally close, and Graham and Stanley would be among Peel's staunchest allies in his government of 1841–6.

Religion, paradoxically in view of the events of 1827–30, enabled Peel to rebuild his shattered party. Defence of the Church of England had been a Tory rallying cry since the reign of Queen Anne. In the 1830s it meant the defence not just of an ecclesiastical edifice but of an established way of life and civilized values. J. W. Croker, a prominent Tory spokesman of the 1820s who refused to stand for the reformed parliament because he believed its members would be urban, radical and uncouth, spoke of the union of Church and State. It symbolized 'that mixture of veneration and love . . . of public liberty and self control, of pride in our ancestors and hopes for our posterity which affects every patient and Christian mind at the contemplation of that glorious system which unites . . . our civil and ecclesiastical constitution'. In 1834–5 the Church seemed in dire need of defence and the Whigs, increasingly tied to radicals and Irishmen, seemed far less likely than the Tories to defend it.

When William IV dismissed Melbourne and installed a minority Tory government at the end of 1834 (see p. 23), Peel used the opportunity to issue a political statement, ostensibly addressed to his constituents at Tamworth, but in reality a national appeal for electoral support. The 'Tamworth Manifesto' would have shocked Lord Liverpool, not in its proposals, but because a prime minister was indulging in such vulgar solicitation for votes outside parliament. This manifesto was a turning-point not just in Tory fortunes but in the nature of the Tory party. Peel for the first time committed his party to accepting the irreversibility of the Reform Act – 'a final and irrevocable settlement of a great Constitutional question' he called it – and also to a programme of moderate reform for the correction of 'proved abuses'. Prominent among the institutions requiring reform in order to preserve their essentials was the Church of England. The only substantial measure which Peel's government of 1834–5 was able to enact was the establishment of an Ecclesiastical Commission. This in due course engendered a string of reforms which strengthened both the morale and the effectiveness of the Church of England during the reign of Queen Victoria.

Peel's primary target in his manifesto was not the 'Ultras'. For the moment they had nowhere else to go. He looked beyond the shires and the small boroughs in search of voters who would see in the Tory party both a guardian of the constitution and a vehicle for cautious, measured reform. The Tories even adopted a new name, which increasingly implied the rejection of mere reaction. Though the word 'Conservative' was, apparently, first used to describe the party in 1830 it came increasingly to be applied to the fusion of the old Tory interest with moderate reformers. The MP Sir John Welsh spelled out the distinction in 1836:

> The Conservative party is not identical with the Tory party. It includes, indeed, the Tories, but it is a more comprehensive term and the basis is a wider one . . . the Conservative party may be said to consist of all that part of the community who are attached to the constitution in *Church* and *State* and who believe that it is threatened with subversion by the encroachments of democracy. . . . They consider that the march of democracy, with its eternal warfare against all that exists, is a retrograde one.

The Conservatives, as we should call them after 1835, made much headway by arguing that their main opponents were indeed flirting with 'the march of democracy'. In the election of 1835, the Conservatives made a net gain of about eighty seats. Virtually all these gains came at the expense of the Whigs rather than the radical elements. In those constituencies where the electorate was radically inclined, principally the populous English and Scottish ones, Conservatism made little headway. Those who were anti-radical and firmly attached to the constitution in Church and State were beginning to see Conservatism as a better guarantor of what they held dear than were the Whigs.

The brief minority government of 1834–5 secured Conservative morale. It also confirmed Peel as the obvious leader and helped to make relations between himself and the Ultras rather less frosty. The manner of the Conservatives' loss of power, moreover, gave great hope for the future. Whigs, O'Connellite Irish and English radical MPs made an agreement in March 1835, known as the Lichfield House Compact, to unite their forces to secure Peel's defeat. Some historians have seen this compact as the true origin of the Liberal party since it implied a definite widening of the landowning Whig party base. Whig landowners, however, remained firmly in charge of all major positions.

Melbourne returned as prime minister in 1835 once the Lichfield House Compact had achieved its objective. The Whig government of 1835–41, however, was frequently embarrassed by its uncomfortably close Irish and radical associations. This became particularly true after the 1837 election when the Conservatives won 313 seats and left Melbourne dependent on O'Connell's support for his overall majority. Such support was suspect in an electorate which was substantially English. The increase in the number of voters by about 80 per cent had resulted in an electorate which was overwhelmingly middle-class and property owning. Over 70 per cent of all parliamentary seats were in England, which worked to the advantage of the Conservatives who were becoming overwhelmingly an English party. They were also helped by the increase in the number of English county seats from 80 to 144, since it was precisely in these seats that the Whigs found it most difficult to hold back the Conservative tide.

Voting patterns emphasize the growing two-party struggle after 1835. To keep the Conservatives out the radicals needed to support the Whigs, and the Whigs, in their turn, became more clearly associated with reform, especially on issues such as appropriation and the desirability of a secret ballot in elections. Just before the election of 1841, William Gladstone, then a rising and committed Conservative utterly loyal to the leadership of Peel, concluded:

> The principle of party has long predominated in this country; it now has a sway almost unlimited . . . [the people] must pin their faith upon some general and leading terms, and by those terms must be defined and determined the great parties which are to contend for mastery in the State.

Voting patterns at Westminster confirmed Gladstone's assessment. Of 594 MPs who sat throughout the parliament of 1835–7, 294 voted consistently Liberal and 273 consistently Conservative. Only 27 voted variably or too infrequently to be classified. No pre-1832 parliament remotely showed this degree of party alignment.

It is tempting to write the history of the Whig/Liberals between 1835 and 1841 in terms of inevitable, inexorable decline. Partly because of the immense presence of Peel, which has attracted the attention of biographers both sympathetic and authoritative, the Conservatives have received the more detailed attention. Yet Melbourne's government deserves more sympathetic attention than it has had. It put in train major administrative reforms, both of the poor law and local government, via the Municipal Corporations Act of 1835. The welter of ecclesiastical and Church reforms passed between 1836 and 1840 are of prime importance. It remained true to Whig reformist traditions and its failing popularity after 1835 was far from uniform across the country. Only in the final years, 1839–41, did its weaknesses assume such proportions as to make its departure a blessing. The Whigs failed to cope competently with mounting economic difficulties which brought higher prices and widespread unemployment. As the financial deficit steadily mounted, even the sypathetic observer Lord Holland noted that it was 'fast assuming the fatal character of Mediocrity' (1).

Peel had the chance to form a government in 1839 when Melbourne offered his resignation after a humiliatingly narrow victory on the Government of Jamaica bill. But he would not accept Queen Victoria's determination to retain certain ladies as members of her household who were known Whig sympathizers, and refused on this account to form a second minority government. Political, as well as constitutional, considerations weighed with Peel in this 'Bedchamber Crisis'. Peel was confident that Melbourne could not revive his party's fortunes if forced to resume office. The Conservative victory, when it came, would probably be the greater in consequence. So it proved in 1841.

The general election of 1841 does much to clarify the respective strengths of the Conservative and Liberal parties. The Conservatives won 367 seats to the Liberals' 291. This healthy Conservative majority rested on a vast superiority in the county seats of England and Wales – 137 to 22. Only five county seats south of the Trent remained in non-Conservative hands. In England and Wales the Conservative majority was roughly 3 : 2 (302 seats to 196). In Scotland and Wales, by contrast, the Conservatives 'lost' the election by 31 to 22 and 62 to 43 seats respectively. Only 2 of Scotland's 23 borough seats were won by the Conservatives.

This election revealed that the true battleground between the parties was the 323 seats representing the English boroughs. Here the Conservatives, aided by some impressive and novel electoral organization, did well enough, though their successes were highly selective. They won seats in established commercial centres like Bristol, Hull, Liverpool and London, but did far less well in the main textile manufacturing centres of northern England like Manchester, Oldham and Halifax. Such places remained overwhelmingly Liberal even in a very good Conservative year. In the sixteen largest parliamentary boroughs, which contained between them half of England's borough population, the Conservatives won less than one-quarter of the seats. As Liberal party managers pointed out, much Tory money had been spent in winnable small boroughs, where bribery and treating of electors remained the order of the day even after 1832. The Liberals were at it too, of course, but with rather less cash and far less success.

The Conservative victory of 1841, therefore, was based on England's counties and smaller boroughs. One further observation, not usually made, puts their triumph into proper perspective. Fewer seats were actually contested (47 per cent of the total) than in any general election since the passage of the Reform Act. Many Conservatives, therefore, gained their seats by nomination rather than by contest. It is clear that the Conservatives in 1841 were the better organized party; it is far from clear that they were the more popular.

The Peel government of 1841–6 is primarily remembered for two things: its series of economic reforms and the manner of its fall. Peel carefully picked professional administrator-politicians for the leading posts in his government. Henry Goulburn became chancellor of the exchequer, the Earl of Ripon (the Robinson and Goderich of the 1820s) president of the board of trade, the Earl of Aberdeen foreign secretary and the two senior 'Dillyites', Graham and Stanley, home secretary and war secretary respectively. It was an experienced as well as an able team, yet Peel's own abilities enabled him not only to control it but to win its unstinting respect.

Government policies were not in themselves novel. They represented a continuation of those begun by the Liverpool government in the 1820s, stressing the elimination of the government deficit, the maintenance of a secure and stable currency, fair levels of taxation upon all sectors of the population which could afford it, and substantially reduced import and export duties. To these ends the famous pieces of Peelite legislation – the reintroduction of income tax in 1842, the free trade budgets of 1842 and 1845, and the Bank Charter Act of 1844 – were directed.

Peel defended his policies on the grounds of national interest. Though much of his legislation anticipated the golden age of classical *laissez-faire* as practised by Liberal governments in the 1850s and 1860s, his view of the role of the government had important elements of the eighteenth century about it. A prime minister, in accepting the monarch's commission to form a government, accepted with it the obligation to govern on broad principles of national security and for the advancement of national prosperity. How did party accommodate itself to this view? Peel saw, with his usual clarity, that the electoral changes of the 1830s necessitated greater party organization and tighter party discipline. He did not accept, however, that party could be anything other than a subordinate element in the constitution. In particular, party considerations should not dictate national policy. This purist constitutional view, allied as it was to Peel's aloofness and a personal shyness which many mistook for detached arrogance, led the prime minister into increasing conflict with his backbenchers.

Peel stressed free trade as necessary in the national interest, but the policy had alarming implications for the majority of his supporters in the Commons. Though Conservatism was a wider creed than Ultra Toryism, the uncomfortable fact remained that most Conservative MPs were, in all essentials, old-style Tories. They represented land; they were staunchly Anglican; they loathed Roman Catholicism; they were deeply anti-reformist in almost every way. Their gratitude to Peel for leading them back to government did not last long. They were uneasy about reductions in duties designed to aid the commercial men whom they distrusted. In 1844, 95 of them voted against Peel on a factory bill which they considered too favourable to the industrialists. In 1845 a more serious revolt occurred over the government's proposal to increase the grant to a Roman Catholic seminary at Maynooth. This was part of a wider strategy to increase propertied Catholic support in Ireland for the Union with Great Britain and to head off nationalism there. It was immensely controversial in England, since anti-Irish sentiment had actually increased since Catholic Emancipation in 1829 because that measure had failed to produce the promised tranquillity in Ireland. Peel, who had deserted the Ultras in 1829, was accused of betraying them again. Half of the Conservatives in the Commons voted against the grant and a Cabinet minister, the young William Gladstone, resigned on the issue.

The internal contradictions of Conservatism had already been revealed, therefore, when Peel took his fateful decision at the end of 1845 to repeal the corn laws. Protection for arable farmers was by now the only substantial block in the way of achieving free trade and the logic of Peel's economic philosophy pointed to their abolition. For landowners and farmers who supported the retention of protection, economics was only a part of the issue. Some certainly believed that they needed protection to survive, but more were swayed by the argument that land was the foundation of society and that landowners also required protection in the interests of social stability and in recognition of their superior propertied status. With the corn laws gone, land would retain no special privileges over trade or commerce. For Tory backbenchers far from certain of the virtues of industrial progress, this was too much to stomach.

Peel's true feelings were expressed best in a private letter to his wife:

How can those who spend their time in hunting and shooting and drinking know what were the motives of those who are responsible for the public security and have access to the best information and have no other object . . . but to provide against danger and consult the general interests of all classes?

When faced with the stark choice of abandoning corn law repeal or breaking up his party, his belief in the subordination of party to considerations of national interest determined his decision. The Protectionists found in Lord George Bentinck and Benjamin Disraeli two vigorous leaders and effective debaters to rally them against the prime minister. When the corn law repeal bill faced its crucial test in the Commons in February 1846 it passed comfortably enough, by 339 votes to 242. But only 112 of those 339 votes were Conservative. Peel had carried repeal by relying on the Whig opposition among whom the issue was far less contentious and whose landowners were, in any case, prodded firmly in the free trade direction by Liberal industrial and commercial pressure from the north of England. This vote broke Peel's party and his resignation followed four months later. It is noteworthy that the support Peel obtained from his own party came much more freely from the larger boroughs. Conservative MPs from these boroughs were made fully aware of commercial feelings on the subject and half of them supported the party leadership. In the Conservative county and university seats, by contrast, 86 per cent of the votes went with Bentinck and Disraeli. The Conservative coalition, painstakingly stitched together by Peel after 1834, had come apart at the seams.

Party organization and identity, 1835–67

Party organization in the constituencies was markedly strengthened after 1832. Local political activity became much more hectic, in part because the Reform Act of 1832 had greatly increased the numbers of men eligible to vote and had also given far more seats to the main centres of population. Two other factors merit consideration. The first was the technical device of the registration of voters and the second the passage in 1835 of the Municipal Corporations Act.

One might assume that all '£10 householders' automatically qualified for a vote in the boroughs after 1832 (1). This was not so. A potential voter had to pay one shilling a year to get his name on to the electoral register. Even then, his qualification might be challenged on a number of grounds, including recent change of address and defaulting on payments of rates. Such challenges were mounted locally in the Barrister's Revising Court. A direct incentive existed for political parties to organize themselves so that the maximum number of known supporters was added to the register and as many opponents as possible successfully challenged. In nearly all the larger boroughs, therefore, parties rapidly established organizations to supervise registration, to disseminate party propaganda and generally to maintain a presence on a scale unknown before 1832. Solicitors generally acted as party agents. They knew their constituencies and they were qualified to present technical arguments at the Barrister's Court where battles could be fierce. In Leeds the electoral revision could not be completed in 1840 because of the number of claims and objections made by the Liberal and Conservative party agents (17).

As frequently happens, the party out of office made most of the running over party organization. In seats with small electorates tight organization was unnecessary. Landlord influence often prevailed over the selection of candidates and getting out the vote was less a matter of canvassing than of insisting upon traditional obligations. Efforts were, therefore, concentrated in the larger seats and several hundred Conservative clubs and associations were in existence by the time of the 1841 election. Centrally, the Conservative Carlton Club was very efficiently managed by Francis Bonham after 1835. An election committee offered advice, circulated propaganda and, on occasion, gave money to the constituencies to fight important seats. Sir Henry Hardinge, who was to serve as secretary of the war department in Peel's 1841 administration, reported from London on the eve of the 1837 general election: 'We have raised here £2400 for Dublin City and £3300 for Westminster – the Candidates and their Committees must do the rest.' A slice of Hardinge's very considerable personal wealth also augmented party funds. He donated £1000 in the early 1830s to 'organize a system of general Management of the Press' (10). Newspaper support for the parties became increasingly prominent after 1832.

A Whig/Liberal organization was built up to match the Conservative one. It had fair success, especially in the boroughs where Liberals and radicals had more promising material to work on than in the counties. The old exclusive Whig club, Brooks's, was supplemented in 1836 by the foundation of the Reform Club in direct opposition to the Carlton. Significantly, it included both Whigs and the less extreme radicals. The Liberal party manager, Joseph Parkes, was a Birmingham man who rapidly established an enviable reputation for shrewdness and efficiency. His record in his own borough was impeccable. In nine general elections held between the first and second Reform Acts Birmingham returned two Liberal MPs on every occasion.

The fact that the large boroughs sent two MPs to parliament enabled the Liberals to present contrasting candidates to the electorate, an Anglican and moderate Whig, for example, teamed with a non-conformist or a radical. The Liberals were a much more heterogeneous party than the Conservatives before the 1870s and they saw considerable advantage in what the Americans call 'a balanced ticket'.

The passage of the Municipal Corporations Act in 1835 imbued local electoral politics in England and Wales with immense vitality. Analogous legislation had similar effects in Scotland and Ireland. Before 1835 most English towns had been ruled by small cliques of self-selecting property owners. They were usually Tory in politics and almost invariably Anglican in religion. The 1835 Act replaced 178 such 'closed boroughs' with a network of borough corporations elected annually by rate-paying householders. It represented a revolution in local government. The free trade radical Richard Cobden enthused that the new corporations would 'deprive the oligarchy of their power in . . . our large towns and . . . put that power into the hands of the people themselves'. His definition of 'the people themselves' was fairly exclusive. Most people who paid rates directly in the 1830s were middle class and Cobden anticipated an invigorating struggle between contending propertied groups. He would not significantly have dissented from the expectation of his political opponent, Robert Peel, that 'the management of Municipal affairs' should be entrusted to 'those who from the possession of property have the strongest interest in good government, and, from the qualification of high character and intelligence, are most likely to conciliate the respect and confidence of their fellow citizens'.

The Municipal Corporations Act gave power to Liberal councillors in most of the larger northern and midland towns. Religion was an extremely important influence on voting behaviour among the middle-class electorate and nonconformists grasped the opportunity of turning out the old, exclusive Anglican elite. The first municipal elections for Manchester and Birmingham, both held in 1838, resulted in the return of no Tories whatsoever. The situation changed rapidly and, while Liberal businessmen controlled most urban councils consistently until the 1870s, the Conservatives were not slow to organize themselves under the new rules and mount powerful challenges. Local organizations with names such as the 'Tradesman's Conservative Association' and the 'Tradesman's Reform Association' joined battle to fight not only the annual local contests but also the rarer parliamentary general elections and by-elections.

Especially before 1867, religion is a much more useful indicator of voting behaviour than either wealth or social class. The substantial majority of nonconformists were Liberals; Anglicans, though with less consistency at least in the towns, tended to vote Conservative. This polarization certainly helps to explain the usual Liberal majorities in the cities. The religious census of 1851 revealed that nonconformist attendances comfortably exceeded Anglican ones in all towns with populations over 50,000, except London. Yorkshire, with its many large towns, had almost twice as many dissenting church attenders as Anglicans. Nevertheless, some Conservative dissenters, most of them Methodists, were found in northern cities such as Sheffield. Similarly, although a majority of successful textile manufacturers were Liberals, a substantial minority were not. In Stockport in the mid 1850s, for example, the largest employers were almost equally divided between Liberals and Conservatives, whereas in nearby Ashton-under-Lyne and Stalybridge virtually all employers were Liberals and most of them nonconformists.

Anti-Catholicism undoubtedly won the Conservatives many votes in northern England from the 1840s onwards. This was particularly pronounced as Irish immigration accelerated rapidly in consequence of the desperation caused by the potato famine in Ireland. Tories were traditionally anti-Catholic and where Catholic immigration was perceived, rightly or wrongly, as a threat to jobs, employment and existing culture, then the Tories benefited. Working-class Orange organizations proliferated in Lancashire in the 1850s; both the 1850s and 1860s saw anti-Catholic riots. Most working men were given the vote in the towns by the terms of the second Reform Act in 1867. They used it in Lancashire to help return 21 Conservative MPs in the general election of 1868 as against only 13 Liberals, and this despite a Liberal overall majority nationally of over 100 seats. Anti-Catholicism also exercised the predominantly middle-class electorate. Liverpool had returned a strong Liberal majority in its town council in the 1830s. The Conservatives won control in the local elections of 1841 and maintained it until the late 1860s, though with their largest majorities in the 1840s when Irish immigration was at its peak. Liverpool, with more Irish immigration than anywhere, was one of the very few northern towns with a Conservative majority on its local council.

Local political activity after 1835 helped to consolidate party identity and allegiance in general elections. Organization and discipline were now at least as likely to be developed locally as imposed from the centre. Local political issues, such as water supply and civic amenities, tended to be much more vigorously and consistently debated than were national ones. Political candidates were also selected on the basis of how well they would represent local interests. Party allegiance in the constituencies remained firm in the later 1840s and 1850s when, according to many accounts, party politics at Westminster were supposed to have been thrown into confusion by the split in the Conservative party over the repeal of the corn laws.

That split was important, of course. It deprived the Conservatives of effective power for a generation. We shall consider below (pp. 46–7) how far the loss of the 'Peelites' (as the free trade Conservatives were inevitably and appropriately called) disturbed the two-party system, but it is clear that it made the Liberals the dominant party. Between June 1846 and December 1868 the Conservative party was in office for only three brief periods: February–December 1852, February 1858 to June 1859, and June 1866 to December 1868. Its leader, until illness forced his reluctant resignation in February 1868, was the Earl of Derby. It was his misfortune to lead three minority, and hence inherently unstable, administrations. His appointment as party leader, and that of Benjamin Disraeli as his chief henchman in the Commons, was almost inevitable. Derby, as Viscount Stanley, had been the only important member of Peel's government to resign on the protection question. The remaining senior ministers willingly saw repeal through and then remained aloof from Derby's Conservatives. With the Peelites went nearly all the Conservatives' expertise and political leadership. Disraeli had proved himself much the most impressive debater on the protectionist side in the Commons and, after a brief and unsuccessful interlude during which Bentinck led there, Disraeli was installed as leader by 1849.

Derby and Disraeli were an unlikely pair of leaders for an anti-reforming party with pronounced reactionary tendencies. Derby's political origins were with the Canningite reforming Tories of the 1820s. He had supported reform in 1832 and had not been warmly received by Conservative backbenchers until the protection issue deprived them of almost every other figure of national stature. He was, at least, an extensive landowner of impeccable aristocratic pedigree (when he succeeded to the peerage he became the fourteenth Earl of Derby) and a convinced Anglican. Disraeli, by contrast, was the son of a Jewish intellectual and had proved himself, since his arrival in parliament in 1837, one of the cleverest MPs around. Neither his religious origins nor his intellectual dexterity were natural qualifications for the leadership of the kind of Conservative party which emerged from the trauma of 1846. The election of 1847 confirmed that the party had retreated in electoral appeal to its English county redoubts. It returned fewer than 230 members; the Peelites, still separate and aloof, numbered almost 100. Derby and Disraeli appreciated that the party needed a far broader electoral appeal if it was to see government again in the foreseeable future.

It is a nice irony that the rebuilding of Conservative fortunes, slowly and painfully in the 1850s and with rather greater rapidity and reward in the 1860s, took place using the lessons which Peel had taught in the 1830s. Above all, the unhappy experience of minority government in 1852 emphasized that the foundation of recovery must be the abandonment of protection. The Conservatives needed to attract industrial and commercial allies, which they could only do by abandoning the very issue which had divorced them from Peel in 1846. They had some limited successes. Improved morale and organization under the management of Philip Rose and William Jolliffe brought rewards during the 1850s. The party won seats at both elections held while the Conservatives were in minority government. In 1852 it won 299 seats (40 of which were lost in the next election in 1857); in 1859 it captured 306, the first time it had achieved 300 seats since Peel's victory of 1841. The borough seats won, however, tended still to be the smaller ones. The Conservatives actually made larger strides in Ireland than in the large boroughs, winning a majority of the seats there for the first time in 1859. Much Irish Catholic disenchantment was evinced with a Liberal party which, under the leadership first of Lord John Russell and then of Palmerston, was proving less sympathetic to Irish grievances than had been hoped.

The two main parties still showed significant differences in social composition. Both, overwhelmingly, were led by established landowners. However, increasing numbers of businessmen and the professional middle classes were coming into the Liberal party by the 1850s. According to an analysis by Professor Vincent of 456 Liberal MPs elected between 1859 and 1874, only about 54 per cent were either large landowners or 'gentlemen of leisure', while fully 30 per cent were businessmen with a further 16 per cent lawyers, some of whom were also either landowners or had additional sources of income (15). By contrast, the Conservative party had only about 20 per cent of MPs whose income and status did not derive primarily from land. Tory members still sat overwhelmingly for county and small borough seats where Anglican clergymen (themselves debarred from sitting as MPs since the established clergy had direct representation in parliament via the bishops sitting in the Lords) were among the most effective, if unofficial, agents and party managers.

The extent to which the Peelite split affected two-party allegiances can easily be exaggerated. Only in the election of 1847 were the Peelites a numerous body in parliament. By 1857 the informed political diarist Greville estimated that 'not a dozen Peelites' remained in splendid isolation from the two-party system. In fact, they had fewer than fifty supporters as early as 1852 since most of the less prominent Peelites quietly rejoined the Conservatives. This process was aided by the Derby government of 1852 and by its commitment not to reintroduce protection. One ex-Peelite, Sir John Pakington, accepted a Cabinet post in this administration. Fortunately for future Conservative fortunes, the protection issue became far less contentious after 1852. It became obvious that the repeal of the corn laws had not destroyed the agricultural interest, as had been gloomily prophesied in 1845–6. Indeed, via the increased investment popularly known as 'high farming' agriculture participated in the rapid increase in national prosperity. The way was thus open for ordinary Peelites, their leader now dead and their cause unequivocally triumphant, to return to the Conservative fold. Most did.

Only initially, therefore, did Peelite numbers, by preventing the election of a government with a Commons majority, contribute to the problem of forming stable administrations. Of much greater consequence was Peelite quality and administrative expertise. Men like Gladstone, Graham, Herbert and Lincoln (from 1851 the Duke of Newcastle) had been almost bred for office. Deprived of it, they chafed and presented what might become disproportionately powerful opposition to any government. Gladstone's savaging of Disraeli's 1852 budget, for example, led to its rejection in the Commons and the first Derby government's resignation. The administration which succeeded it was a coalition of Whig/Liberals and a small but crucial number of Peelites. It was led by the Peelite Earl of Aberdeen.

If they broke the Conservatives in 1852, they had contributed significantly to maintaining Lord John Russell's Liberal government in office during the preceding six years. With what must have seemed intolerable superiority, the Peelites sustained a government they considered short on both ability and direction largely because they feared that the alternative would bring instability and the possible reintroduction of protection. Though the Russell government had few substantial achievements to boast, it did accelerate the movement towards complete free trade by abolishing the Navigation Acts in 1849. A substantially increased state grant for education in 1847 and the passage of a Public Health Act in 1848 could be represented as consonant with Whig reformist traditions. The government showed few concessions to its middle-class support. Twelve of the twenty-one members of Russell's cabinet were aristocrats or the sons of aristocrats; five more had inherited baronetcies.

The government was forced to resign in 1852 when Peelites refused to support it further after the passage of Russell's anti-Catholic

47

Ecclesiastical Titles Bill. The government had already been weakened by the open rift between Russell and his independent-minded and aggressive foreign secretary, Viscount Palmerston. The lack of amity and trust between these two senior Whigs – 'those two terrible old men' as Queen Victoria later called them – contributed rather more than did the behaviour of the Peelites to the ministerial instability of the 1850s.

The Aberdeen coalition which followed the short Derby ministry lasted little more than two years before collapsing under the strains imposed by the outbreak of the Crimean War against Russia. During 1853, however, it provided ample evidence of its Peelite provenance. Gladstone, the new chancellor, was firmly in the 'liberal Tory' traditions discernible as early as the peacetime ministry of Pitt and followed through by Huskisson, Robinson and Peel. His budget offered the prospect of consistently low public expenditure, a balanced account and, in the conditions of prosperity and free trade which such policies were designed to stimulate, the eventual abolition of income tax. Increased wartime expenditure after 1854 invalidated its central assumptions, but the budget belonged to the classical school of liberal economics.

A Liberal government under Palmerston succeeded Aberdeen's and lasted exactly three years, until February 1858. It won the Crimean War and it traded mightily on the prime minister's reputation for handling foreigners with no more respect than they deserved. The 1857 election turned on personal support for Palmerston as a man who would not shrink from using British strength against those who challenged British interests, however trivial. Other prime ministers since Palmerston have discovered how potent an electoral concoction patriotism can be, especially when presented in populist terms. In 1857 it served to win the Liberals more seats than at any election since 1835, even though many fastidious Liberal and radical politicians were aghast at the crudity and tub-thumping emotionalism of the prime minister's direct appeal to the people.

Despite the lack of a parliamentary majority the Conservative government of 1858–9 had some modest successes. It abolished the necessity for MPs to have property in order to stand for parliament, thus opening the way for the first working men to become MPs sixteen years later, and it also permitted practising Jews to sit in parliament. It was brought down in circumstances similar to those which defeated Peel in 1835. Opposition politicians came together to agree upon a strategy to turn the government out. A meeting held at Willis's rooms in June 1859 brought an agreement that the various radical groupings would work together for a common objective – never an easy task; Palmerston and Russell finally sank their personal differences; Gladstone and the few remaining Peelites threw in their lot with the Liberals. Gladstone had been much courted by both Liberals and Conservatives at various times during the 1850s. He bridled almost equally at working with Disraeli, whose apparent lack of principle he abominated, and with Palmerston, whose populism and chauvinism were almost a standing affront to elevated Peelism. By 1859, however, Gladstone at last found that he could work with Palmerston on the basis of agreement over British attitudes to nationalism in Europe. Gladstone was also doubtless exercised by the more self-interested consideration that, if he finally rejoined the Conservatives, he would contest the succession to that party's leadership with Disraeli, who was only five years older. The Liberals were led by Palmerston, who was seventy-five in 1859, and Russell, who was sixty-seven. The fifty-year-old Gladstone could not afford to parade his separatist Peelite credentials indefinitely. The successful outcome to the Willis's room meeting was the passage of a no-confidence motion in Derby's government. Palmerston, rather to Queen Victoria's annoyance since she suspected his motives as thoroughly as did Gladstone, became prime minister once again in an administration which would last until the old man's death in 1865.

After 1859, Peelism was no more. This political truth was given physical emphasis by the deaths, between 1860 and 1864, of four of its most senior practitioners – Graham, Aberdeen, Herbert and Newcastle. Gladstone, though now securely in the Liberal camp, was the last guardian of an honoured tradition. Party politics assumed a stable aspect with a Liberal majority of about 40 seats over the Conservatives, an advantage which would be increased to over 80 at the general election of 1865, held three months before Palmerston's death. Few could disagree with Walter Bagehot's assessment, made in 1860, that in relation to parliament, party was 'bone of its bone and flesh of its flesh'.

Little disturbed the domestic policy of Palmerston's last government. Gladstone, chancellor of the exchequer once more, was able to lower taxation again after the dislocating effects of war and to reduce public expenditure by about 10 per cent between 1861 and 1866. Virtually all remaining duties were abolished by the budget of 1860. The final abolition of newspaper duties in 1861, which lowered their price and increased their availability, began a process whereby Gladstone became known as the 'People's William' and the working man's friend – both unlikely sobriquets for the 'stern unbending Tory' that T. B. Macaulay had described in the late 1830s. Parliamentary reform, the only seriously contentious question, was shelved while Palmerston, a known opponent of the idea, lived.

Russell's determination to pass a further measure of reform when he succeeded Palmerston as prime minister briefly disturbed the two-party system but did not shake it. Russell had been one of the more radical members of Grey's government during the first reform crisis of 1830–32, and he had failed with three measures to extend the franchise in 1852, 1854 and 1860. The question turned on the extent to which it was wise to admit working men to the franchise. Because of the effects of gentle inflation between the 1830s and the 1860s, about one-quarter of the male working class already qualified via the household franchise. Many Liberal politicians, including nearly all radicals and the non-radical Gladstone, were now prone to declare that working men had earned the right to vote because of their contributions to the economy and their manifest lack of revolutionary zeal. Russell's reform bill of 1866 was modest enough, involving reductions in the voting qualification in both counties and boroughs, and some further disfranchisement of small boroughs. However, it ran into serious difficulties with the right wing of the party who engineered an adverse vote in the Commons in June 1866 which led immediately to Russell's resignation.

As it happened, the Liberal anti-reformers (known as the Adullamites) had jumped from the frying pan into the fire. Derby wearily took up the cudgels of minority office for the third time and was determined to have something to show for it. Disraeli took the view that Conservative success in enacting reform when the Liberals had failed was crucial for morale within the party. Although what the bill contained could hardly be irrelevant, and should be made if possible to work in the Conservative interest, the details were less important than the fact of a *Conservative* Reform Act. The Conservative proposals were much amended as they passed through the Commons and ended up by being far more extensive than originally envisaged. The Reform Act gave the vote in the boroughs to all tenants and most lodgers with a residence qualification of at least twelve months. Working-class votes would henceforth determine the fate of many urban constituencies in an electorate which was virtually doubled overall.

For a generation after 1867 these new working-class electors would cast their votes dutifully for one or other of the two established parties. That they did not rush to form their own is testimony, among other things, to the stability of the mid-Victorian constitution. In its essentials, the British political system of 1867 was not only stable but recognizably modern. Important adjustments, of course, had still to be made. No woman would cast a legal vote in a parliamentary election until 1918. The Labour party would rise after 1900 and the Liberal party decline spectacularly after 1918. This changed the players, not the nature of the game. By 1867 both Lords and monarchy had accepted subordinate positions in the constitution. The struggle for power concerned control of the House of Commons and it was waged between two political parties possessing surprising degrees of organizational cohesion both at Westminster and in the constituencies. The arbiter between them was the general election, at which the opinion of men possessed of at least modest means was canvassed. In 1867 it was deemed safe to consult even those of less than modest means.

In 1868 Benjamin Disraeli, now prime minister, established what has since become a tradition. Having lost the general election of that year to Gladstone and the Liberals, he resigned almost as soon as the results were known. Unlike his predecessors, he did not wait to meet parliament and face inevitable defeat there. His instincts were sound. He appreciated that there were no independents whose votes could be wheedled in parliament or whose minds could be changed by seductive oratory. He also knew that Queen Victoria could not help him. Our study began in 1783 with a monarch, George III, who dismissed ministers he disliked and successfully installed in William Pitt a prime minister of his own choosing. It is appropriate, therefore, that it should end with a monarch forced by the choice of the electorate to part with a prime minister she admired and to accept as his successor a man, William Gladstone, whom she disliked intensely. By his actions in 1868, Disraeli publicly acknowledged the effective sovereignty of the electorate. It was also a symbolic recognition that the modern political system was in being.

Appendix

British prime ministers and administrations, 1783–1867

The party labels attached to these administrations are in no sense official. The terms used are sometimes my own and need to be used in the context of the text. They are included in the hope that they will help students to grasp something of the intricacies of party groupings when these are complex.

WILLIAM PITT THE YOUNGER		1783–1801
(a) Court Whig 1783–94		
(b) 'New Tory' 1794–1801 – coalition of old Pitt supporters and conservative Whigs under Portland		
HENRY ADDINGTON (later Viscount Sidmouth) Includes Portland Whigs and some Pittites	Tory	1801–4
WILLIAM PITT THE YOUNGER Most Pittites and Portland	Tory	1804–6
LORD GRENVILLE 'Ministry of all the Talents': Whig-dominated coalition plus Sidmouth	Whig	1806–7
DUKE OF PORTLAND Portland Whigs and Pittites	Tory	1807–9
SPENCER PERCEVAL	Tory	1809–12
LORD LIVERPOOL Pittite base and Sidmouth. After 1822 Grenvillite Whigs join	Tory	1812–27
GEORGE CANNING 'Liberal Tories' plus some Whigs	Tory	1827
VISCOUNT GODERICH Same grouping as Canning after Canning's death	Tory	1827–8
DUKE OF WELLINGTON Mostly 'Protestant Tories' and Ultras	Tory	1828–30

52

EARL GREY	Whig	1830–34
Whigs and some Canningites		
VISCOUNT MELBOURNE	Whig	1834
ROBERT PEEL	Conservative	1834–5
VISCOUNT MELBOURNE	Whig	1835–41
ROBERT PEEL	Conservative	1841–6
LORD JOHN RUSSELL	Liberal	1846–52
Established Whigs in leading ministerial positions		
EARL OF DERBY	Conservative	1852
EARL OF ABERDEEN	Peelite	1852–5
Coalition of Liberals and Peelites		
VISCOUNT PALMERSTON	Liberal	1855–8
EARL OF DERBY	Conservative	1858–9
VISCOUNT PALMERSTON	Liberal	1859–65
LORD JOHN RUSSELL	Liberal	1865–6
EARL OF DERBY	Conservative	1866–8
BENJAMIN DISRAELI	Conservative	1868

Further reading

Place of publication is London unless otherwise stated.

General texts (all available in paperback)

1 E. J. Evans, *The Forging of the Modern State: Early Industrial Britain, 1783–1870* (Harlow, Longman, 1983) – covers the whole period and includes lists of all Cabinet Ministers and general election results.
2 I. R. Christie, *Wars and Revolutions: Britain 1760–1815* (Edward Arnold, 1982).
3 N. Gash, *Aristocracy and People: Britain 1815–1865* (Edward Arnold, 1979).

Studies of party

4 F. O'Gorman, *The Emergence of the British Two-party System, 1760–1832* (Edward Arnold, 1982) – brief but trenchant and controversial.
5 B. W. Hill, *British Parliamentary Parties, 1742–1832* (George Allen & Unwin, 1985).
6 F. O'Gorman, *The Whig Party and the French Revolution* (Macmillan, 1967).
7 A. Mitchell, *The Whigs in Opposition, 1815–1830* (Oxford, Oxford University Press, 1967).
8 A. S. Foord, *His Majesty's Opposition, 1714–1832* (Oxford, Oxford University Press, 1964).
9 J. E. Cookson, *Lord Liverpool's Administration, 1815–1822* (Glasgow, Scottish Academic Press, 1975).
10 R. Stewart, *The Foundation of the Conservative Party, 1830–1867* (Harlow, Longman, 1978) – in fact begins before 1830 and is a very impressive study.
11 R. Blake, *The Conservative Party from Peel to Churchill* (Fontana, 1972).
12 E. J. Evans, *The Great Reform Act of 1832* (Lancaster Pamphlet, Methuen, 1983).

13 D. Southgate (ed.), *The Conservative Leadership, 1832–1932* (Macmillan, 1974).

14 D. Southgate, *The Passing of the Whigs, 1832–1886* (Macmillan, 1962).

15 J. R. Vincent, *The Formation of the Liberal Party, 1857–68* (Constable, 1966).

16 J. B. Conacher, *The Peelites and the Party System, 1846–52* (Newton Abbot, David & Charles, 1972).

17 D. Fraser, *Urban Politics in Victorian England* (Macmillan, 1979).

Biographies

18 J. Ehrman, *The Younger Pitt* (Constable, 2 vols, 1969 and 1983).

19 N. Gash, *Lord Liverpool* (Weidenfeld & Nicolson, 1984).

20 N. Gash, *Sir Robert Peel* (Harlow, Longman, 1972).

21 R. Blake, *Disraeli* (Eyre & Spottiswoode, 1966; University Paperback, Methuen, 1969).

22 R. T. Shannon, *Gladstone*, vol. 1, *1809–65* (Hamish Hamilton, 1982; University Paperback, Methuen, 1984).